A Sunset Book

Garden Pools Fountains & Waterfalls

By the editorial staffs of
Sunset Books and Sunset Magazine

LANE BOOKS · MENLO PARK, CALIF.

Leon Frehner design

Gardens are places to nurture memories, to spend tranquil moments with the peaceful reflections of trees in water. In this case, Mahonia repens creeps gracefully along huge boulders at the feet of water birch and smooth sumac. These stones and plants are native to the high Rocky Mountains near Salt Lake City.

CONTENTS

THE COVER: The pool shown at top left was designed by Stanley Bitters, and is described fully on page 14. Photo is by Ernest Braun. At bottom left is a free-form concrete pool designed and built by Herbert Bess; the waterfall is powered by a vertical pump hidden beneath a concrete slab to the left of the main pool. Traditional fountain-pool at top right is supplied by a garden hose coupled to an aluminum tube that projects from below-water pedestal of cupid figure. Pool at bottom right, designed by Kathryn Imlay Stedman, has a small pump that forces water through a series of small plastic tubes cast into the painted concrete shell. The latter three photos by Hubert L. MeckLen.

Eleventh Printing April 1971

 LIBRARY OF CONGRESS CATALOG CARD: 65-15208. TITLE NO. 122. LITHOGRAPHED IN THE UNITED STATES.

John Robert Baker design

In a dry climate, this pool with its short stream was made wide and shallow for maximum cooling effect. Pool was poured with aid of forms; rocks were set in wet concrete to restore some of natural effect.

Why put a pool in the garden?

Water is the difference between green mantled hills and wind drifted desert sand, the difference between teeming cities and vast unpopulated landscapes, the difference between prosperity and some meager existence.

Water is the essential medium for a man who lives from one fishing expedition to the next, and anathema to the mythical American boy on the brink of his bath.

Water is a frequent element in gardens, where it serves to recall a variety of pleasurable times.

A hiker in the towering Western mountains may enjoy the haunting memory of a clear, granite-bottomed lake, encountered once on a day of unparalleled weather. He might use a small pool carefully planted to evoke a fleeting impression of that day.

Another man may remember a pond in farm country, always perfectly smooth, always full of fish, always a place to go and sit and be calm. He might attempt something like that.

Yet another man may recall a great formal garden, surrounding a great house. From that garden he might choose to build a brick or tile-

L. Raymond Hodges design

Metal tank end painted black and buried provides a reflecting pool for moisture-loving plants around it.

At left: Vigorously splashing falls create opposite mood from that above. A sump pump produces the torrent.

edged pond with water lilies floating on its surface and goldfish prescribing lazy arcs just beneath the surface.

Or it may be nothing as sentimental as all that. It just may be that a good-sized garden pool will round the landscape design of one garden, or save unwanted labor in another.

It may be that a sizable body of water will help to cool down the patio on hot, dry days in summer.

It may be that the lady of the house would like to have some water handy because she wants to grow some plants that insist on keeping their feet wet, or it may be that some clean-limbed trees would be enhanced if reflected in the mirror surface of a pool.

On still another hand, it might be merely a case of water arriving in the garden as a by-product of an interest in some hobby. Fish-keeping and concrete sculpture come readily to mind in this connection.

Whichever of these factors brings water to the garden, the experience usually turns out to be an enjoyable one for the recipient. Getting the water into the garden in the first place can be at least interesting, if not an unmitigated pleasure as the work goes forward. A variety of alternative methods is offered in this book.

Cast on sand mold, this concrete reflecting pool is easy to make, and easy (well, relatively anyway) to move about the garden. Painted dark blue to aid narcissus behind in admiring their reflections.

Water as a decorative accent

Water in small amounts usually serves some decorative purpose in a garden. It is placed in a showy bowl, or it is an excuse to fashion a large-scale mosaic piece, or it sets off a prize plant.

The tiny pools spring about half from craftsmen and half from ingenious scavengers-about in attics and garages.

Concrete long suffered from its reputation of being a utilitarian material, good for streets, warehouses and other pragmatic projects. In recent times, though, its great plasticity of form won it new admirers. The advent of lightweight gravels such as vermiculite, haydite, and others, made concrete a still more likely product for craft projects. Also, concrete plays a graceful host to mosaics.

The simpler bowls require almost no special supplies beyond the basic ingredients. Few tools are needed, and previous experience is not a requirement for success. Some standard methods are described in detail on pages 10 and 11.

Small pools of this type can be made either of standard concrete, using granite gravels, or of lightweight concrete, using one of the gravels noted above. The merits of one choice or another are primarily matters of taste, since either type of concrete will hold water as well as the other.

As the pictures demonstrate, one of the chief charms of these tiny pools is portability. In the cases of all but the smallest pools, the lightweight concrete weighs enough less to make its use worthwhile to the family that rearranges its

Chinese rice-pounding bowl can be imitated with lightweight concrete cast on sand. This one harbors water lettuce in a cool place.

At right: Dramatic combination of reflected sky and real driftwood rewards he who pauses to look into this bowl of cast concrete, which is too small for plants, fish.

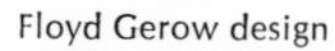
Floyd Gerow design

patio decorations often enough. Also, the surface of lightweight concrete resembles stone more closely than does standard concrete.

On the other hand, standard concrete will make a smoother finish surface with less effort, a slight advantage when algae finally come to cloud the waters. Smooth concrete is easier to clean and to keep clean. Smooth surfaces take paint and waterproofing compounds more readily, too. (A finish coat over lightweight concrete will serve the purpose; the formula is 1 part cement to 1 part clean sand.)

Seekers of salvaged pool forms have demonstrated that almost anything capable of holding water can, with suitable surroundings, become an attractive garden pool.

Among other contemporary artifacts, these are proven: Photographer's darkroom trays, army surplus plastic lens, bonsai bowls, furnace ducts, oil drums, wine barrels, laundry tubs, horse troughs, and hot water (and other) tanks. There is no reason to assume that enameled dish pans, wheelbarrow beds, and galvanized buckets would do less well.

Small pools of this type do have limits. They are ill-suited to keeping fish or water plants. The small amount of water in them can change temperature too fast for the health of either kind of life. (There are exceptions to each, shown in this chapter.) Sinking the pools below grade will help to stabilize water temperatures.

Such pools work best around a grouping of container plants, or in a small, groomed garden where they can draw attention to a subtle bloom, or serve as a miniature reflecting pool. To be most effective, they should be placed on or near patio furnishings, or close to walkways or garden paths where the viewer can focus closely on what he sees.

Eight feet across, this pool is barely portable. One can be cast in place on a sandy bed edged with stakes driven tightly together in the ground. See page 57.

Kaye Scott design

Leftover sheetmetal bent into a semi-circle made this pool, which is painted inside and out.

Kent McCoy design

Tank ends are a popular type of salvaged pool. Garden hose hidden in plants provides active play of water—spillage is of no matter in this case.

Chinese frying pans (two of them) made the form for this pool. The method is described on page 10.

Mrs. Clark H. Gates design

Florence Swift design

Weighty patio table is cast concrete with metal hoops embedded in its surface to form shallow pools. Pebble mosaics dress up the pools.

Lana Christensen design

Study in textures includes smooth water, gravel, driftwood, huge green bottle, lace-leafed plants. Pool is a metal tank end sunk to brim in gravel.

Frances Callahan design

Old laundry tub sunk nearly to its rim harbors both goldfish and waterlilies in comfort. Both fish and plants must be thinned regularly to avoid crowding.

Virginia Russell design

Corrugated metal strips around the edges of a sand mold gave these pools an added fillip of formality. A ¼-inch copper tube fit to garden hose supplies water.

1. **Reinforcing** mesh shaped into form before any concrete is poured. Mesh should end inch short of outer edge.

2. **Pour concrete;** trowel into layer half as thick as finished bowl. Then place reinforcing. Finish pour.

3. **Set clamps** to hold forms firmly. Fill top form with stones, or place some other compressive weight.

4. **Special clamp** holds two halves of mold in rigid relationship, to produce a machine smooth bowl.

5. **Trim excess** away from edge with ordinary kitchen knife to obtain smooth effect shown on page 8.

6. **After concrete** hardens, remove form carefully, bottom form first. Allow about 48 hours before this step.

7. **Bowl rests** on wagon for trip to spot where it will cure. Inner form left in place as insurance.

8. **Wrap bowl** in burlap, and keep burlap damp for several days so concrete will cure properly before use.

Decorative pools of cast concrete

Compression molds are particularly worthwhile when a landscaping scheme calls for several repeats of a single design, or when the pool is to have a highly finished appearance.

In this series of how-to photographs, the mold is two Chinese *woks*, 32 and 28 inches in diameter. Their smooth metal surfaces produce pools of almost machine-made smoothness and evenness. (One of the pools is pictured on page 8, lower right.) Further, an adventurous cook gets the benefit of the *woks'* presence in her kitchen once the pool project is completed.

Other forms might be found or made. The only requirements are that the curves of the two parts be similar enough to avoid too-thin places in the cast bowl, and that they be of a hard enough material with a clean enough surface to avoid having the project and its mold become inseparable. Metal or wood will serve the purpose if the facing parts are brushed with light, clean crankcase oil, or some similar lubricant.

The *woks* used for this project have special brackets welded to their edges to guarantee an even mold. *Woks* and brackets together cost about $30. Ordinary C-clamps might be substituted for the special brackets. The clamps will be less easy to handle, but will serve adequately and cost less.

Haydite is the aggregate used in this project. The absolute amounts were: 1½ buckets (10-qt. bucket) of cement, 1½ buckets of sand, and ½-bucket of Haydite. About eight quarts of water will provide a good, stiff mix if the sand is only damp to start. Use less water if the sand is especially wet.

Rougher-hewn circular pools can be made expediently with a mound of sand (and perhaps a ring of sheet metal to hold the sand in place) as the mold.

The main parts of the system are a rod at the center, anchored top and bottom, and a wooden template which revolves on the axis provided by the rod to form first the sand, then the pool itself.

The sand which forms the mold should be saturated so it will pack hard, and so it will not suck water from the concrete mix, weakening it.

This project resulted in the small fountain shown on page 13 (top, left). The formula was 1 (cement) • 2 (sand) • 3 (aggregate), using ½-inch mesh Haydite as the aggregate. After the bowl was cast and separated from the mold, the craftsman applied a 1 • 1 finish, then a water-seal.

1. Wood template shapes sand in a rough circular form fashioned from kraft paper, wood stakes.

2. Shovel concrete onto damp sand and trowel into a layer of roughly even depth. Place reinforcement.

3. Add concrete to cover wire mesh thoroughly. Rough trowel the wet mix into place.

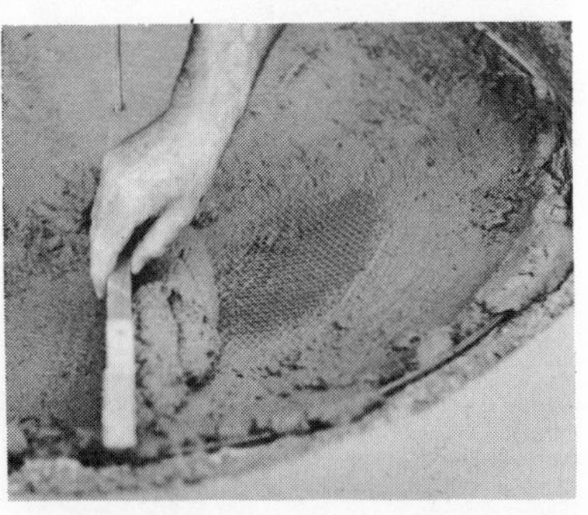

4. Use template to achieve final inner surface for bowl. Jogging will produce smooth surface.

A compression mold can be used to gain any kind of shape for which molds can be found—generally regular geometric shapes such as circles or rectangles. A sand mold, used alone, will produce rough-hewn approximations of the same shapes.

For the altogether fanciful, ingenious carpentry is necessary. This single example uses sand and a bottomless box in combination to produce concave rectangles. From this base point, quick trowel work adds shape to the bowl areas.

But this is only a start. The boxes can go on to become as complex as the craftsman wills. Hardboard is flexible enough (warm it first) to produce curving surfaces. Sheet metal will bend in all directions, too.

For free-form efforts such as this, use haydite in a 4•2•1 or 4•3•2 ratio. Keep water in mix to a minimum, so the mix will stay in the desired shape once trowelled.

1. Tamp sand into any desired curve or plane within confines of lightly tacked wood frame.

2. Shovel concrete into forms, using gentle motion to avoid disturbing sand. Try for fairly even spread.

3. Trowel mix into finished shape quickly, with as few strokes as possible. Over-working causes cracks.

4. Knock down form with light hammer taps on protruding "ears." Scoop sand away from hardened concrete.

Philip Gilmore design

Main basin of this pool is concrete cast in a form. The small fountainhead pieces are lightweight concrete cast with copper tubing cast into them. The tubes are welded to larger tube leading from small pump.

Ideas for decorative fountains

Getting water into motion removes it from the role of spear-carrier and gives it a meatier part to play in a garden's decorative scheme. Yet, creating a fountain need be only slightly more difficult than finding or making a bowl to hold still water.

It is always possible to tap off a regular cold water line to make a garden fountain. In cases where the fountain is used infrequently or the overflow can be drained away or put to secondary use, this is a satisfactory method. Pinching the supply line's tip or capping it will produce the jet effect.

In most cases, however, and in all the cases shown in this section small, inexpensive recirculating pumps are used. The tiny, 1/55hp pump will lift 200 gallons of water per hour to a height of one foot, an adequate supply for each of the examples shown on these two pages, and for most of the examples shown in this chapter.

Commercially manufactured fountainheads form sprays ranging from simple jets to complex water sculptures. Some of these effects can be approximated with home-built systems, and many more combined effects of rising and falling water are open to the man who will experiment with multiple spray heads, catch basins, splash surfaces, and other devices that interfere with the simple forces of gravity.

Smallest pump available is housed in box below cast concrete "stone" with hole drilled in it. Return tube cast into bowl, which is foot in diameter.

Lawrence Halprin design

Similar fountain to one above, except that return tube and fountainhead are side by side in pool floor. For note on pebble mosaic, see page 58.

Lawrence Halprin design

Larger scale, permanent location distinguish this fountain from other two on page. However, the recirculating pump assembly is fundamentally similar to the others. See p. 14.

Stanley Bitters design

Leaves of slate (with a hole drilled in each) fit over inlet pipe of fountain. Water burbles gently out of pipe, becomes a fine spray as it falls from leaf to leaf.

Water in fanciful motion

The basic engineering solution for a fountain is shown in the small photo below. A number of variations are to be found on page 63. Whether a pump is attached to the bottom of a container or is housed separately, the main point is to keep it below surface level so the pump will not lose its prime, and because most pumps push water up better than they pull it up.

Another prime point to remember is that the higher the water must be pushed by the pump, the less force it will have to make a spray. The most forceful spray will emerge from a short inlet pipe with a small opening at its tip. The laziest stream will emerge from a long pipe with a large opening. The heaviest stream will emerge from a large opening just beneath the water's surface. Using small-diameter tubing reduces the efficiency of the pump, as it increases the amount of friction between water and pipe. For maximum efficiency, use the diameter pipe that fits the pump's outlet.

Heavy column of water in this fountain is produced by terminating the inlet pipe below the surface of the pool.

Tiny pump attached to bottom of plastic pan shows how simple the plumbing of a small fountain can be.

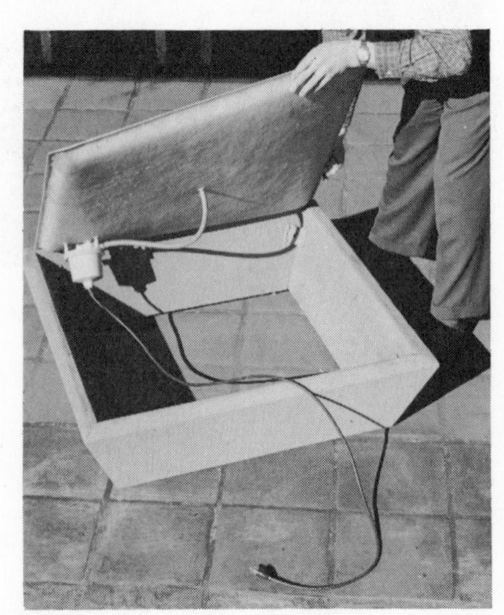

In design, the main ground rule is: Use a short, heavy column of water in windy spots. Go for distance and drama where the spray will not blow overside, dousing all hands to lee.

Most designers attempt to place a fountain in a way that causes the spray to stand out from its background. Water in a spray tends to be a translucent white, so most backgrounds are dark. Fine sprays tend to be most visible against flat surfaces. Heavy sprays will stand out from even a lacy bower of leaves.

A point easily overlooked in the planning and building of a small fountain is the location of the pump for easy access. The machine is a simple one, but it will need occasional maintenance. With a portable fountain of the type pictured, problems seldom arise. With fixed fountains, though, the effort should be made not to hide the pump so thoroughly it cannot be reached without tearing up the patio or the fountain itself. (Submersible pumps do away with the entire difficulty.)

Eckbo, Royston & Williams design

A welded whirlimagig throws water in whimsical patterns above a commercially available metal bowl. Special nozzles at the tip of each pipe produce the jet effect.

In placid entry garden, a small spray plays above a metal pool. This bowl is very much like the one above right.

Lawrence Halprin design

Cast concrete pool on pedestal is brightened by pebble mosaic. See next page for one construction method.

Georg Hoy design

Virginia Davidson design

Huge sand mold produced this fountain, which is gracefully proportioned, yet rough-hewn enough to fit in any casual patio. Use of carefully carpentered forms would produce evener results shown on page 19.

1. Mark circumference of pool with chalk tied to measured length of string. Check radius with template.

5. Excavate for pipes and footing. Dimensions shown in sketch below. Seat pipes, then pour footing.

Fountain built on a sand mold

This graceful raised fountain cost its builder a pile of sand, a wooden template, about $50 worth of building materials, and a weekend of diligent work.

The required materials are these: 100 pounds of cement (white cement can be obtained for a premium price), two tons of builder's sand, 150 pounds of $\frac{1}{2}$-inch pea gravel, 10 feet of $\frac{3}{8}$-inch copper pipe, 10 feet of $\frac{1}{2}$-inch copper pipe (both of these may vary, depending on the pump's location), a 5-gallon watertight container to hold the pump, a 60-cycle submersible pump, and 40 feet of $\frac{1}{2}$-inch steel rods.

Also needed: a 3-foot length of 1 by 4-inch lumber, a 7 by 10-inch piece of $\frac{3}{4}$-inch plywood, two 4-inch mending plates, and two small cans of the kind used for frozen concentrates of fruit juices.

Piping and footing: After locating the fountain, the first task is to set the pipes in the ground and pour part of the footing.

The footing is a block of concrete about 2 feet square. It prevents the fountain from tipping. Dig the footing hole about 14 inches deep. At the same time, dig a trench for the pipes from the footing hole to the point where the pump will go.

Bend the pipes to a 90° angle, taking care not to make the corner too abrupt. The vertical section of the pipes should be long enough so it will stick up three inches above the finished floor of the pool.

Lay the pipes in the trench. Check the vertical section with a spirit level to make sure it is perpendicular. (Otherwise, the

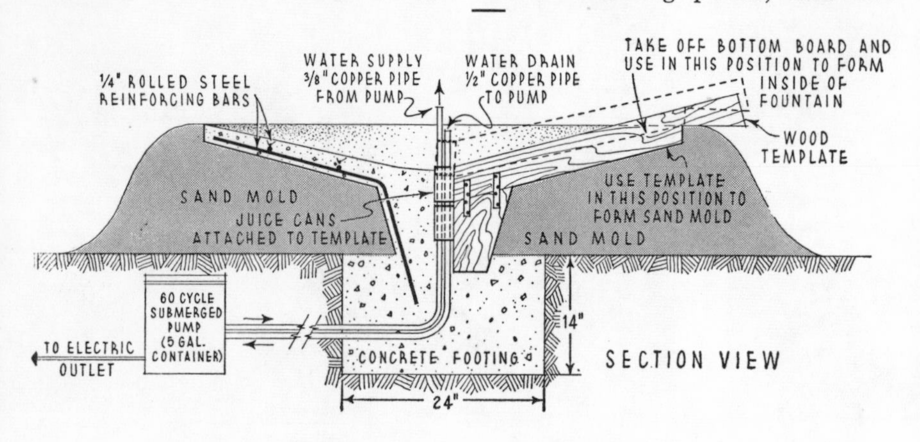

2. If on patio, break out hole for footing. For a fountain of this size, hole should be 24 by 24 inches.

3. Using scribed circle, cut and bend reinforcing rods to fit as described in text below.

4. Small frozen juice cans make suitable sleeve for template to revolve upon. Exact fit is best bet.

6. Build sand mold, using template to achieve shape. Axis should be precisely vertical to avoid tilted pool.

7. Pour concrete to half the thickness of pool, then embed reinforcing rods. Intersections should be wired.

8. Finish pour. Remove ear from template. Use it to jog either rippled or smooth surface into inside of bowl.

template will not work correctly.)

Mix enough concrete to fill the bottom 8 inches of the footing hole. Allow concrete to harden overnight so pipes will offer a solid pivot to the template.

Template and reinforcing: While the concrete is setting, the template can be made and the reinforcing rods cut and bent.

The template is shown in the photos above.

As reinforcement, this design calls for eight 3-foot sections, each bent to match the template, and two circular rods. One of the circular rods should fall three inches from the edge. The other should be about one-third the circumference (Circumference = radius × 6.2148).

Building the mold: The second day, pour the remaining six inches of the footing, bringing it to ground level. Make this portion of the mix dry enough to support the weight of the sand, but soft enough to receive the reinforcing rods at a later stage.

Now, build the mold by piling wet sand under the template, keeping even on all sides at all stages. Keep the sand wet and compact it with hand pats or by jogging the template.

Pouring the concrete: Mix the concrete 1 part cement, 1 part sand, 1 part gravel, and about 1 gallon of water to each 100 pounds of aggregate.

Remove the template; pour concrete into the middle of the mold, over the footing area. Trowel from center to edge in one direction only, so sand is not disturbed. Cover the entire mold with a 1-inch layer of concrete. Embed the steel rods in a spoke pattern. Put the circular rods down, wiring them to spokes with light wire and keeping the whole assembly flat. Pour another 1-inch layer of concrete over the reinforcing grill. Remove the bottom section of the template, and use the straight edge of the top to smooth the bowl.

Trim edges smooth before the concrete sets.

Keep the fountain damp for two days while the concrete sets. When it has set, fit the fountainhead on the feed pipe. In this case, the designer used a threaded pipe cap, with three holes drilled to receive three lengths of 3/16-inch copper tubes which were welded in place and fitted with nozzles.

Cut the ½-inch return pipe to water level; cover it with a copper screen to filter out dirt.

The pump is connected at the other end according to manufacturer's specifications.

Clyde Childress design

Negative forms make useful empty places, as in this case. The most important step in making a fountain of this kind is the planning of drip basins' relationship to each other. Preliminary sketch is the easiest method.

1. Cover bottom of mold with sand. Bend ¼-inch rod for pool projections. Wire together. Bend mesh over them.

2. Drive rods in ground. Pour inch of concrete. Position hose. Cover with mesh. Pour 3 more inches of concrete.

3. Cover bottom layer with inflated balloons. Work more concrete under, around sides until balloons covered.

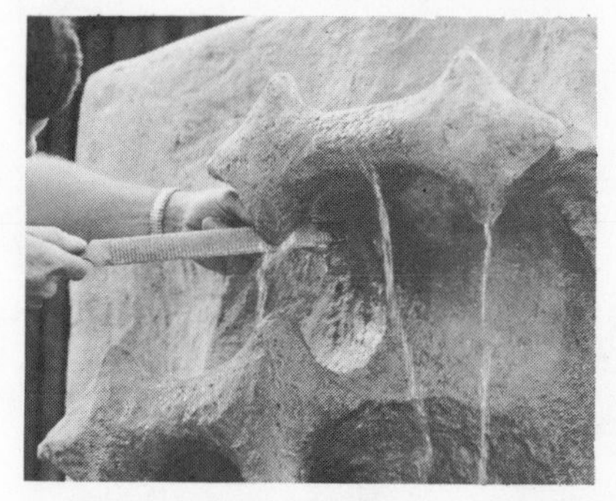

4. After curing, remove unwanted parts. Trim and form with wood rasp. Use wire brush to finish.

Using 'negative space'

Water bubbles gently from a hose buried in the back slab of this fountain, and runs in rivulets with a soft splashing sound to a pool at its base.

The fountain was cast on its back as a slab with a three-dimensional grille on top. It was cast of vermiculite concrete (2 • 2 • 3), reinforced with metal mesh and ¼-inch steel rod. Water-filled balloons (the heavy, 10-cent kind) formed the mold for the grille. After the concrete had set, the balloons were emptied and removed.

This fountain took 3 cu. ft. of vermiculite, 1½ cu. ft. of cement, and 1½ cu. ft. of sand, plus ¼ cu. ft. of fireclay (which makes the surface easier to mold.) It stands nearly 5 feet high, and is slightly less than 4 feet wide at its base.

The hose is cast in the slab with its coupling protruding from the bottom at the back. The top end emerges from the front at the center of the topmost catch basin. It is trimmed flush with the face of the slab after the concrete has set.

The concrete can be worked easily after it sets but before it cures. It is at this point that the grille is altered to its final form. Obviously excess parts can be chipped away from the grille. Then set the fountain up to try the water flow. Get rid of high spots with a wood rasp. Build up low spots with a special mix of 1 part cement, 1 part sand, and fireclay (one-eighth as much fireclay as cement). Before adding this, brush the surface to be built up with a thick slurry of cement and water.

Once the grille pattern is satisfactory, the whole surface can be smoothed with a wire brush.

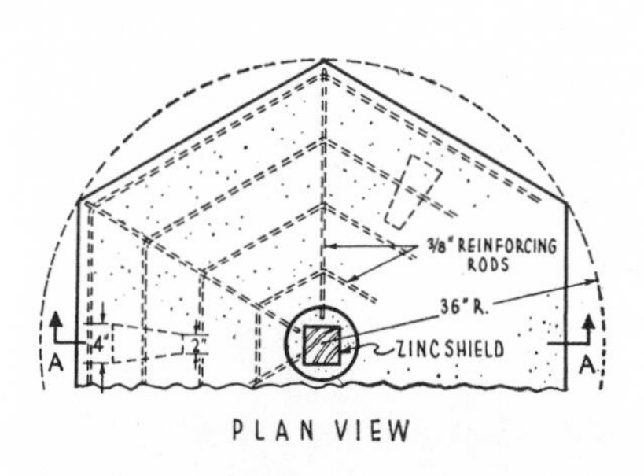

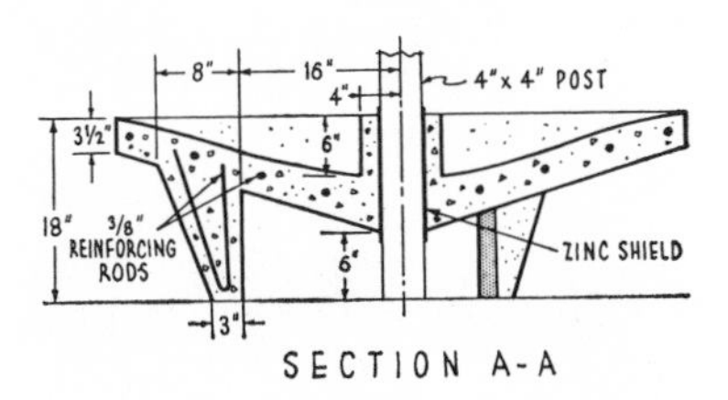

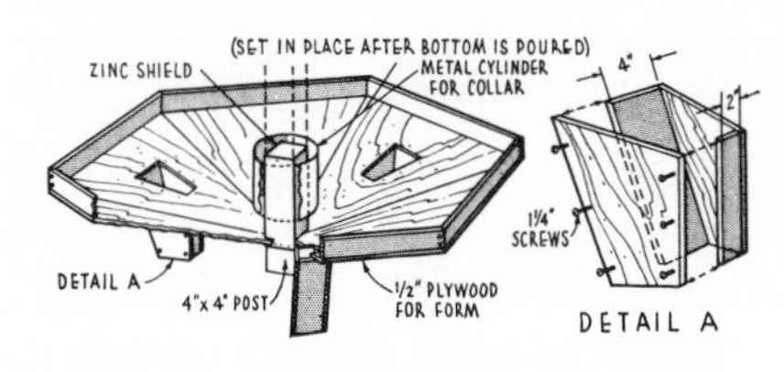

Fine sense of geometry produced this basic idea, and high skill in carpentry brought the fountain into being. Each bowl is one-third smaller than its next lower companion; each is six-sided.

Charles B. Shaw design

For skilled craftsmen

Here is a project for a man with woodworking skill—and confidence. Plywood forms were used so the corners would be precisely sharp.

As the sketch above indicates, fitting the legs to the main pool form was an exacting task. Also, the forms (of ½-inch plywood) needed considerable shoring up to bear the weight of the concrete even though a lightweight aggregate was used.

The formula was 2 parts cement, 2 parts sand, 1 part fireclay, and 4 parts aggregate. The aggregate, in turn, was 2 parts ⅜-inch Haydite to 1 part fine gravel.

Over this the craftsman applied a finish coat of 1 • 1 sand-cement, to assure the fountain's being waterproof. This coat also contained about ¼-pound of integral dye to color the finished product.

Zinc flashing, applied with mastic, protects the wooden post against deterioration. The ¾-inch galvanized pipe supports and drains for the two upper pools were cast right in the concrete.

Water is pumped to the top of the upper pipe, and flows down through the pipe to drilled holes near surface level in the top pool. The water flows from pool to pool until it reaches the lowest. From there it drains through a tube (buried in the planting bed) to the recirculating pump.

The roundabout system was designed to retain the free-floating appearances of the upper two pools.

Bettler Baldwin-Owen Peters design

Asymmetry serves to distinguish "formal modern" from "formal traditional" in this case. Two raised sides oppose two level sides, while random concrete cylinders in water complete the unbalancing act. Pool is cast concrete shell.

Traditional pools and fountains

Europe's great gardens of almost every age used pools and fountains of enormous size. The Victorians of England built palatial homes for goldfish. The Romans used stair-step pools and fountains to cool hot summer nights along the Mediterranean. The French spread enormous sheets of water out before the chateaux so admirers could reflect upon their enjoyment.

While it is nearly impossible to maintain gardens on that grand scale in modern cities and suburbs, the basic ideas behind pools and fountains of earlier times are as good as they ever were. Goldfish dimpling the waters of a pool still make a pleasant sight. Hot, dry summer days and evenings still can use the cooling effect of moving water. Fine homes and gardens still cast delightful reflections.

The orderliness of the formal garden of yore still has its attraction for many contemporary homeowners. Gracefully proportioned geometric shapes well-used can produce an air of tranquility in a garden as readily as any other landscaping device. Thoughtful choice of materials can recapture something of an earlier era, or can match the most spare and utilitarian product of contemporary architecture. The focal point provided by a garden pool makes a natural starting point for a new garden design—and becomes too obtrusive to ignore once built.

While contemporary Americans do not get on as famously with geometry as did the ancient Greeks, it is still a sound procedure to pay strict attention to scale (height as well as width and length), and to placement in the garden.

C. Jacques Hahn design

In luxuriantly planted patio, a sunken pool makes focal point and reflecting surface for prized plants. Metal fish fountainhead is tied into regular garden water line.

Jack Gibson design

Sheetmetal inside form allowed casting of "grand piano" water basin within rectangular pool form. Metal tank end on pool edge is planted with alpine miniatures.

Alexander C. Prentice, Jr., design

Enormous open expanse of deck is broken by this raised pool, which is made of a concrete shell faced and capped with brick. Papyrus grows in open-bottomed well.

Traditional pool designs

In a Victorian garden, the pool was often a generous circle or rectangle, slightly raised, set in the center of an area, and surrounded by spacious walks so it could be viewed from every side. But the enormous and enormously fussy Victorian garden failed to survive the disappearance of a patient, pipe-smoking professional gardener with quarters above the coach house. A few gardens are still large enough to accommodate such pools, but in most cases the pool has to be set near some border if there is to be enough room for something else. It is the choice of brick, fitted stone, or tile used in a simple shape that recalls the old style.

The ruddy face of brick is a warm and familiar friend in formal gardens. A raised pool with brick walls provides a traditional framework for water lilies floating within its borders, and it is at least as pleasing to goldfish as any other commonly used building material.

But brick serves equally well in a modern context. Bricks-in-sand patios, with sunken pools,

Walter & Florence Gerke design

Concrete shell faced with brick, capped by tile nestles at foot of retaining wall, a relief from expanses of concrete in patio. Plants in corner add soft quality as they swirl around a jumble of volcanic rock.

Pool in brick patio is cast concrete. Patio bricks are set in sand, except for edge row around pool, which is set in concrete. Rocks, plant pockets enhance informality.

Lawrence Halprin design

crop up regularly in contemporary surroundings.

One of the greatest advantages of brick is its inherent patterned appearance. Brick can be used gracefully in any amount, large or small, so it is somewhat less difficult than other materials to keep in proportion to its environment. The regular unit lends itself to modular design ("modular" means that a certain square unit is set up, and that all elements within the design use that unit as a base; multiples of it allow for variation).

Amateur bricklayers can come to grief with brick if they use it to form the walls of a pool. It takes well-made, well-laid mortar to escape leaks in a wall with so many mortar joints. A professional can be expected to succeed, although even a professionally-laid wall will need two coats of a commercial waterproofing. Bricks are too porous to do the job unaided.

Many homeowners who doubt their skills as bricklayers will use poured concrete to form a shell, and face the above-grade portion of the shell with brick, or they will mount a brick rim atop the concrete walls of a sunken pool.

Concrete blocks sometimes do a similar job better than brick, especially where they have

E. Dillman Morris design

Concrete block pools need carefully made mortar joints and water seal coats to make them watertight.

Thomas Church design

Even rooftop gardens can have small pools. This one is a concrete shell, the depth of two courses of bricks.

already set the tenor of a garden through use as a foundation or in a garden wall. Their greater size means fewer mortar joints per square foot of surface, and they can be faced with tile, a mosaic design, or even brick. They are easier to reinforce than brick because of their hollow cores.

Poured concrete has its evident advantages. It is the most plastic of these materials, as well as the most impermeable. Its utilitarian character can be hidden with paint, or a facing of brick, tile, or mosaic. Its forms can be lined to produce special effects. For example, an outside-facing wall can be given a strong light-and-shadow pattern by lining the outer form with grapestakes. (It is not so advisable for an inside wall if the pool is to hold fish and plants—the crannies only offer footholds for algae.)

Concrete does have some material disadvantages. It is heavy to work with. It uses carpentered forms, which are seldom easy to manufacture. It requires considerable post-operative care; the surface has to be kept damp for at least a week to allow it to set. There is an excess of lime in concrete, which therefore has to be cured before fish or plants can live in the water

One way to waterproof a concrete block pool is with a pebble or other mosaic. The mortar bed guarantees watertightness at the floor-wall joint.

Nel Sinton-John Bolles design

Eckbo, Royston & Williams design

Difficult but rewarding is the free-form pool, almost always made of cast concrete. A form of this complexity usually will be made of some sheet material.

Walter & Florence Gerke design

Combined forms of rectangle and circle call for masterful handling of quarried stone, especially if pool walls extend considerably above grade as in this case.

held in a new pool. The latter process usually takes at least 10 days. (The others have to be cured, too, but less time is needed.)

Avoiding later troubles

Whichever of these materials finally comes to make the pool, a few general conditions apply to the design.

Sunken pools need some kind of lip to keep surface water from running into the pool during rains. At worst, in a drainless pool, overflow can drown a few plants near the pool and can float goldfish overboard with fatal consequence to them. At the least, in a pool with an overflow drain, the waters can be muddied.

An inch or two of wall above the ground will do. Also, a gravel-filled drain all around the pool will take care of water draining along the surrounding surface. Such a drain can be hidden under grass. It should be about eight inches wide and a foot deep.

The question of whether or not a pipe drain is desirable in a pool is an open one. Most pools need a light cleaning each spring and fall. The lack of a drain means the pool has to be siphoned or pumped empty for cleaning, so any chemicals used in the cleaning will be hard to flush from the floor of the pool. Most homeowners, looking over their individual situations, will be able to decide if siphoning is a practical enough solution to make a slight savings on drain installation.

Safeguarding toddlers against garden pools is not easy. One method is simply to build a raised pool; children big enough to climb up onto a wall can be expected to have some regard for water. The other is to set a screen on pegs just a few inches below the water's surface. The pegs can be cast into the walls when the pool is built. The screen—a large-mesh one is best—is secured to a pipe framework, which then rests on the pegs.

Eckbo, Royston & Williams design

Concrete blocks set off upper section of pool; cast concrete forms the main body, which is strewn with river rock to make a better home for goldfish. In upper part, sunken terra cotta pipe sections house dwarf Umbrella plant. The main body of the pool is 18 inches deep, ideal for the fish which live in it. Water lilies offer shade for them.

Fish and plants seem little bothered by such contraptions, which are barely visible in water suitable for aquatic life.

Pools suitable for plants and fish should be at least 18 inches in depth. One expert recommends 24 inches as ideal.

Of course the pool can be divided into sections to provide for plants. There can be a deep pocket in a generally shallow pool, or an interior pocket can be filled with earth to within an inch of the surface for bog plants, while another segment is kept free of earth for true water plants or purely for appearance. Both of these solutions are demonstrated in photographs in this chapter.

Plants and fish both like sunlight. The minimum amount they require is four hours a day, and more is advisable. For this reason, pools should not be located under trees. Also, the leaves of deciduous trees release a gas when they decompose under water; the gas is harmful to both fish and plants.

Interlocking triangles are basic design figures for shallow pool, which has deep trough at foreground to accommodate culture needs of water lilies.

Eckbo, Royston & Williams design

Osmundson-Staley design

First step was placing of drain tile. Concrete poured into carefully excavated floor, allowed to cure for week; drain pipe cast in place. Walls are double rows of stretchers, with vertical reinforcement.

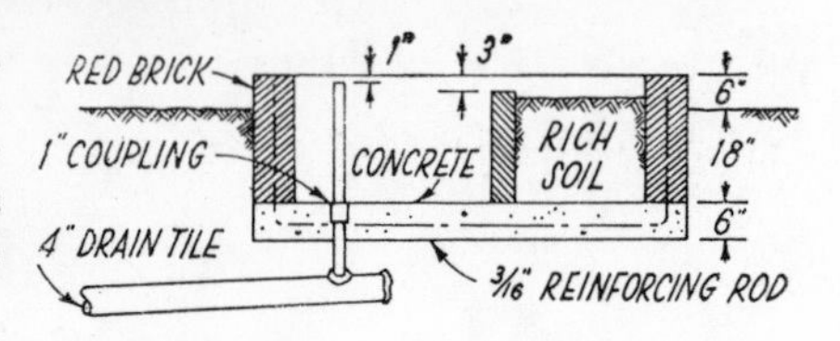

Osmundson-Staley design

Curved wall is self-reinforcing, but mortar joints are hard to make well. Joints are wedge-shaped; bricks should be set correctly on first try to avoid leaks later. Water lilies are in wood planter set on pool floor.

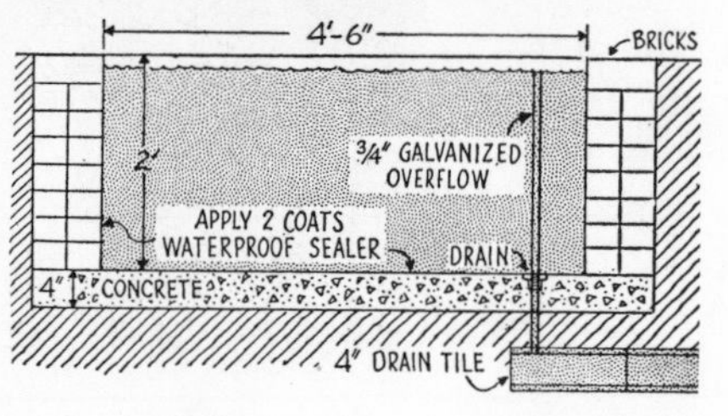

Using bricks or blocks

Laying up the amount of brick used in a small garden pool is a fairly simple task in terms of physical labor.

There are some complications. A curved wall is self-reinforcing, but uses wedge-shaped mortar joints which are not easy for a novice. A straight wall must be reinforced with metal rods. (See page 58.)

Except for this difference, the main points in each of these pools are similar.

The first step is careful excavation to prepare for the pouring of a concrete floor. The deeper trench, to contain 4-inch drain tile, should disturb the compacted dirt floor of the excavation as little as possible.

Once poured, the floor needs only two days to set before brick walls can be laid up—but only if the mason does not work on the floor. It needs at least a week before it is set and cured sufficiently to bear the weight of a man working.

Typically, below-grade brick walls are made of double rows of "stretchers" (bricks laid end to end), to make a wall 8 inches thick. A top course of "headers" (bricks laid side by side), as in these photos, will fit atop this type of wall, which is the easiest to lay up. (It also takes vertical reinforcing most easily.) The rolok bond is also used.

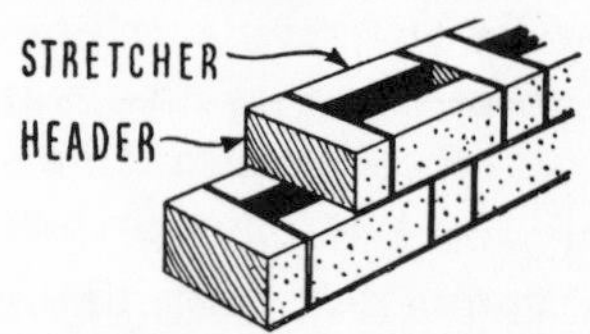

The first course is laid in a bed of mortar ½-inch thick. Subsequent mortar joints are all ½-inch.

Finished walls require two coats of waterproofing compound.

Using concrete in forms

Form-poured concrete stands as the most-used pool, fountain, or waterfall material in contemporary-style gardens. The nature of the material allows it to be as formal or as informal as the forms which shape it. The two examples demonstrated here are, in turn, carefully formal and relaxedly informal.

Each uses standard 1 • 2 • 3 (cement, sand, aggregate) formula concrete.

The topmost pool is made in two pours, with a two-part form of bent ⅛-inch plywood (it could also be hardboard). The outer form is set and held in place with 2 by 4-inch stakes driven 10 inches deep.

The first pour provides a 4-inch thick floor, broken only by planter forms.

As soon as the pour is completed, trowel the top smooth. (For added durability, reinforcing rods in the floor are an advisable step.) Then place the second part of the form. As the sketch shows, this form is braced internally, and suspended from ears that hold it at the chosen height and in the established relationship to the outer form.

The second pour brings the pool walls to their final height.

For a below-grade pool, the method shown in the lower photo avoids the building of carpentered forms. It sacrifices precise edges, and also increases the possibility of a separation in the joint between walls and floor.

The method is this: With a post-hole shovel, dig a trench four inches wide, to the desired depth. Line the inside wall with asphalt paper, and pour concrete to fill. The following weekend, excavate the interior of the pool (with great care), and pour the floor.

Osmundson-Staley design

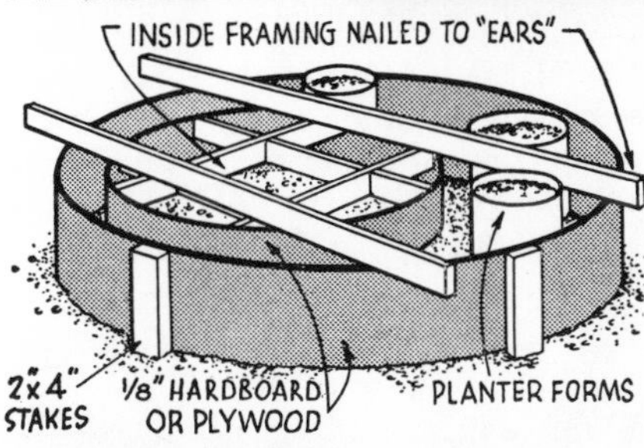

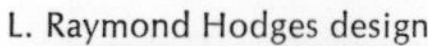

Key factor in achieving desired design in this project is placement of inside form. Since it hangs from ears, marks on the ears and outer form will guarantee correct placement. Stops would be better.

L. Raymond Hodges design

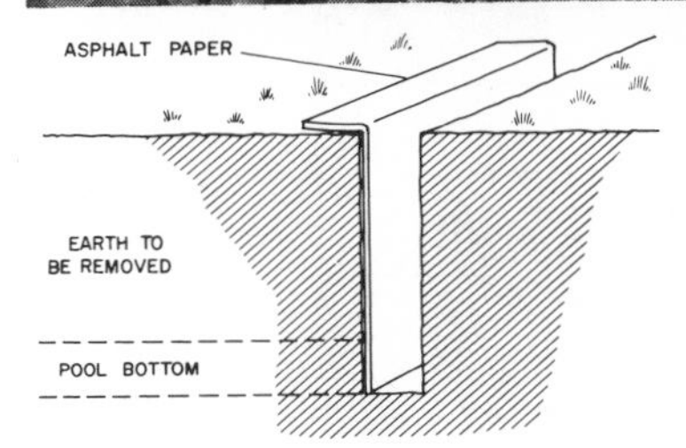

Asphalt paper buckles and bends enough to guarantee a certain informality in finished edges. A man wishing more regular edges on wall tops could use staked lengths of 1 by 6 along with the paper on inside edges.

Guy Greene design

In desert country, broad expanses of moving water can help cool a patio. A recirculating pump moves water from the lowest section of this pool up to the spill pan (top center of photo). Overflow from basin passes through main pool, then courses through drain tiles set in brick wall above the sunken section of the pool.

Far less formal pool (in cooler area) uses similar technique to pool above; water splashes noisily on rocks. A cluster of horsetails hides more of brick wall.

Courtland Paul design

Formal fountain designs

First the Greeks and the Romans, and later the Italians and Spaniards incorporated moving water into their gardens and courtyards as a cooling device against the Mediterranean sun.

Their ideas using multiple shallow pools continue to have application in the original areas, and in wide ranges of California, Arizona, Eastern Oregon, Nevada, and Eastern Washington, and wherever else summer heat is dry enough for evaporative cooling to take place.

Pools of this kind require a relatively large amount of space. The one pictured at the lower right on page 29, for example, is 21 feet long and 7 feet across, hardly adaptable to a handkerchief garden.

Where space is at a premium, fountains do much better at providing the same kind of relief from dry summer heat.

But beating the heat is a mere practical reason for building a fountain, or a two or three-tier pool. The simple pleasure of having moving water in the garden is both a visual and an audible one worth having for itself.

Certain complications ensue from the choice of moving as opposed to still water. The plumb-

John Wegman-Robt. Offenhauser design

Metal spill pans are commercially available in a variety of forms. Some are designed to fit recirculating pumps. Some can be bought in ready-to-use "kit" forms.

Thomas Church design

Rotating head on inlet line sends water spiralling upwards above surface of pool in **Sunset's** patio. This solution more pleasing to eye than ear.

ing chores grow more complex, and the design must in part bow to the needs of fish or plant life if the builder elects to include them in the pool, too.

Water on the move needs some kind of power. The choice between a mechanical pump and the existing pressure in a municipal water system is almost entirely dependent upon design conditions. The cost of electricity required to operate a typical garden pump is usually about equal to the cost of water tapped out of the household supply and run off through a fountain and pool.

One obvious factor is the capacity of a pool to drain. Sometimes water can be allowed to flow out to a low patch in considerable volume, allowing regular, fairly long-term operation of the fountain. This may be as much as the pool's builder desires. In other cases, it may be easy to tie into the main drain for the property, allowing endless operation of the fountain.

The man who wants plants or fish in his fountain, however, must use a recirculating pump. Both forms of life require "aged" water. This means that the water must be slightly acid, and it must have food in it. Municipal reservoir systems in most Western communities provide alkaline water that is chemically treated to kill the elemental life on which both fish and plants are dependent for their own existence.

Against brick wall, water spouts then falls on sounding board before continuing its noisy descent through two more pools. Perforated pipe makes multiple spray.

Osmundson-Staley design

Robert Dhaemers-Kitchen & Holt design

Welded steel walls of this pool were cast into concrete retaining wall, patio floor. Water is pumped up into clusters of copper "leaves"; it sprays through them.

Floyd Cowan design

Metal fish sculpture embedded in brick wall spouts water supply into a small lily pool made of brick.

H. P. Weidman design

Moisture-loving plants surround pool supplied from garden water line. Lack of drain requires this solution to overflow problem. "Drip-stones" on wall add audibility.

A recirculating pump, by oxygenating a constant supply of water, actually aids the fish and plants in a pool.

The number of approaches open to a man who wants some action out of the water in his pool is almost limitless.

Literally hundreds of manufactured fountainheads are on sale in garden supply stores and other dealers in plumbing and hardware supplies. These send water upward in every shape from a massive column to a lace-like spray.

An ingenious handyman can create sprays of his own by perforating pipe, or by welding jets to pipe or tubing. Copper is easiest to work, but should be avoided if fish are to live in the pool; it is poisonous to them in any but small amounts.

Special effects for falling water

Falling water is falling water; it is the surface from which it falls that occupies most of the attention of a designer. A striking number of variations are demonstrated on these two pages. The appearance of the falling water from one example to the next is not greatly different, but the sound produced by the different approaches does vary noticeably.

The great number of brass leaves in the photo

Williams & Williams design

Rigid rectangles of metal produce the same amount of sound as stones set in wall above pool on facing page.

Henry Van Siegman design

Another variation on the theme is series of bowls. Pump returns water from lowest bowl to spout set in wall.

Osmundson-Staley design

It looks like the same idea as those above, but is not. Triangular metal sheets are offset, so water flows off each separately, straight into pool below. Equalizing valve between outlets insures balanced flows. (See p. 63.)

at the left of page 30 produces hundreds of tiny streams of water falling from differing heights. A soft hissing sound results, much like that of a spring rain on a lake surface. The opposite sound is produced by the lower right photo on the same page. A heavy stream cascades from stone to stone on the face of the wall, finally plunging into the large bowl. The net effect approaches the chuckling sound of a granite-bottomed stream.

The other "falls" are audible, but even greater emphasis is placed on the formal appearance of the whole structure.

In most of these cases, a very small pump returns the water from the main pool to the top of the fall. The volume per second is not large. When this is the case, flat elements can be equipped with a shallow lip, which will store enough water to produce an even sheet across the width of the tray. Where two outlets exist for a single falls, an equalizing valve at the outlet nearest the pump will guarantee a flow of water to the farther outlet.

Where fish are to live in the pool, some care should be taken to design the falls in a way that will leave a sizable area of calm water. Neither fish nor plants enjoy a constant drumfire of turbulence.

Paul Hamilton design

Burr Richards design

Huge, tile-lined bathtub has mirroring pool beyond glass, in private garden. Underwater containers in corner hold iris, papyrus, water lilies. Pool open to sky.

Small, free-form sunken pool in corner of private garden outside bedroom is host to moisture-loving plants, is used mainly for reflecting lantern, plants.

Semi-circular pool is similar to that pictured above, if not so closely tied to bathtub. Easier to build for being below-grade; more difficult for curving wall.

Charles Montooth design

Pools for private gardens

The obvious location for a garden pool is out where everybody can enjoy it. A less obvious, potentially more pleasing location for a pool is in a small, private garden outside the master bath or bedroom, where it can help provide an air of tranquility for the adults in a family.

In each of the three examples shown in photographs on this page, the designers made clear efforts to link outdoors with indoors. Indoor tiles go through glass walls uninterrupted. The shape of the bath tub is repeated in the pool. There is no change in level between inside and out.

Structurally, the pools are no different than others described in this chapter. In the cases of the pools which abut a glass wall, some thought might be given to the amount of work required to keep the glass clean. The cleaner the water in the pool, the easier that job will be. Failing clean water in the pool, a "splash board" at least four inches high will help if rain can fall directly into the pool. Fountainheads should be far enough away to avoid spattering, too.

Joe Lamb design

Cascading pools alongside patio stairs are only part of a complex of moving water. Recirculating pump returns water from pool at foot of stairs to another pool near garden bench at rear of patio. Water flows under patio to head of stairs, then down to bottom pool as shown in photo. Swimming-pool pump powers the system.

Cascading pools

Both of these cascading pools require great volumes of water by garden standards. Both use ½-hp swimming pool pumps (which are self-priming, and can be used above surface level of the water) equipped with screen filters.

The rate of descent for a cascade of this type can vary to a considerable degree, depending on water volume. The tile-lined pools in the lower photo drop about one foot in a linear distance of 31 feet; the pools alongside the stairway dip at a faster rate.

In both cases, three walls of each pool are about four inches deep, while the wall over which water spills is only two inches deep. The front lip insures an even flow of water, and also traps dirt and other foreign matter.

In the upper photo, each pool has a dirt-floored planting pocket, as does the main pool at the bottom of the stairs. The pools shown in the lower photo are used to clean the surface of a swimming pool.

Tile-lined pools step down in series. These were made to aerate water, clean surface of small swimming pool, but idea adaptable to any terraced area.

Eckbo, Royston & Williams design

C. Jacques Hahn design

Large pool in Japanese garden is made of concrete, poured without forms and trowelled into desired shape. Edges are obscured by heavy plantings, stones, other devices. All of these aspects are common with "natural" pools.

Natural pools and waterfalls

What is "natural" water in the Western context? It is no easy question to answer. There are rushing streams on granite mountains, lazy streams in upland meadows, muddy streams in farm valleys, and all of these come in large sizes and small. There are glacial ponds high in the mountains, weed-choked ponds on farms, spring-fed lakes, river-fed lakes, tidal lagoons.

In a garden, a "natural" pool, waterfall, or stream is almost any body of water that has no square corners, no perpendicular walls, no man-made edges in sight, and which does have native stone or soil close around it along with native plants, or at least plants so common to the area that they seem native.

From that point forward, an astounding variety of choices belongs to the designer, who usually finds himself inspired by some pool or stream that is fondly remembered from a vacation or from some earlier home. It may be an alpine pool. It may be a willow-shaded pond. Or it may even be a tiny spring at some desert oasis.

The difficult task is not in casting the simple shell of reinforced concrete that holds the water. For most, the difficult task is in achieving a sense of scale and a sense of fitness within the confines of an urban or suburban garden. Some solutions to these problems are shown in the chapter; almost all are the products of landscape architects or other highly trained designers.

Louise Bell design

George Murata design

Impression of nature rather than a straight copy of it, this pool is frankly man-made, but with enough character to fit into an informal (and desert) garden.

Roland Hoyt design

Calm, tropical waters are one "natural" effect. Showy plants surround simple concrete shell. Stones stacked around plant box in pool's center; they circle edge, too.

Low-growing trees hide the fact that this stream's source is rather abrupt, at the foot of property fence. Such attention to illusion helps "naturalness" of garden pools.

William Steward design

Free-form concrete shell was designed especially to hold fish. Uphill sides designed to exclude runoff from rains, a winter problem. Summer heat causes evaporation loss of about 1 inch in depth each week.

1. Rubble backfill strengthens wall. Floor excavated to assure general depth of two feet required by fish.

2. Stakes in grid pattern showed how deep to pour concrete. These were removed as pouring reached them.

3. Concrete was tamped down around grid pattern of reinforcing rods to eliminate all air pockets in floor.

4. Heavy rocks were broken, then reassembled with mortar once in place, to avoid rolling them across floor.

A big pool designed to hold fish

Even though the foot of a hill made a natural site for this 16 by 32-foot pool, its construction required several weeks of the property owner's time. The builder worked alone on all phases of the project except for the one day required to pour the concrete, when a willing neighbor and the builder's teen-age son added muscle.

Gently sloping ground formed three sides of the pool. The fourth side was built—stone atop a heavy concrete footing—and then backfilled with concrete and rubble to make a gentle slope along the fourth "shore." Some excavation was necessary to get a deep enough basin.

A level for the built-up wall was achieved with the use of a water-filled transparent plastic garden hose (when the water stands even below each upraised tip, the hose is level).

On the uphill side, a 1 by 6-inch redwood board supported by stakes served as a perimeter marker for the concrete pour.

Stakes driven into the ground in a grid pattern established a 4-inch depth for the concrete floor. These were removed one-by-one as the pouring progressed to them. The stakes at the uphill side were set one inch lower than the top of the rock wall.

A drainage ditch, eight inches wide and a foot deep, encircles the grade-level parts of the pool. It carries off drainage water, avoiding overflow in the pool, and muddied water.

The concrete is standard formula transit mix, sealed with a ¼-inch sealer coat of 1 part cement, 1 part sand. Commercial waterproofing topped that, in two coats.

Free-form concrete for natural effects

On a much smaller scale, this pool uses the same technique as that on the facing page. It is one of the easiest ways to make a small, informal or natural pool.

The builder used a fairly stiff mix of 1 part cement, 2 parts sand, and 3 parts gravel. The pool is poured in one continuous operation, and since the sides approach closely a slope of 45°, concrete has to be stiff to stay in place.

The mix is troweled into shape as it is poured. In this case, the builder started at the tip so he could work carefully toward the drain and inlet pipes (the inlet pipe was capped with plastic to keep it clean during the building process).

To aid the natural appearance, the pool surface was covered with a rock mosaic, which was set in place while the concrete was still plastic. The mosaic extends from the edge of the pool to the bottom curve of the wall; the floor was left exposed and rough.

This pool is located in a mild-winter area, so its builder did not take the precautionary step of putting down a three to four-inch layer of compacted gravel as a base for his concrete shell. In cold areas, this technique will minimize the thaw-season possibility of heaving and settling soil, which can cause even reinforced concrete to crack.

The excavation was made with care so that the concrete does rest on firmly compacted soil. Trenches for pipes were kept as small as possible, and they were filled with gravel. (A recirculating pump produces the small waterfall; its system is separate from the drain, which is controlled by a valve outside the pool.)

Lawrence Halprin design

Water gurgles cheerfully through a fissure in the stone wall behind this pool. A medium-sized recirculating pump imitates the artesian effect. Mature plants will mask the raw edges. Edge is higher than grade-level.

1. Pump, drain pipes set in narrow trenches at bottom of excavation for pool. Plugged to keep out dirt.

2. Trenches covered. Drain grate marks level of finished pool floor. Outer form is staked hardboard.

3. Stiff mix shoveled into form, troweled to rough finish as quickly as possible because of Step 4.

4. Rock mosaic around walls of pool required very fast work to stay ahead of setting concrete.

Nagao Sakurai design

Finicky attention to detail made this authentic Japanese garden a world of its own, set as it is next to a huge Tudor house. Stones, stone lanterns, plants that reflect showily in the water are all a part of the garden. The pool is large, and its water is aerated for fish by means of a hidden recirculating pump system.

The Japanese influence

The influence of Japanese gardens, like that of Japanese architecture, has made itself felt in the West for a long time. But it is usually only bits and pieces of the Japanese style that find their way into an American garden.

Wisely so. A full-scale Japanese garden is a major investment, and a major alteration to the appearance of a house and its site. In addition to being major, it is most difficult to change without going back to the beginning. George Schenk, in his **Sunset** book, *How to plan, establish and maintain Rock Gardens*, advises his readers: "The American homeowner can with great profit absorb the essence of Japanese gardening and accept its basic elements of stone, water and foliage in quiet arrangement. But for the protection of his property investment, he

Mario Corbett design

Admixture of oriental garden and occidental patio works well as a unit. The patio is higher than the pool, so it is separated enough to retain its own identity. The pool is at least part in shade at all times, ideal for fish since temperature variations are minimized. **Below:** Detailed view of shoreline shows how stones, plants hide concrete.

should be chary of installing a formal Japanese rock garden, complete with stone lantern. He should wait and ruminate a good long time—three years, perhaps—before deciding how far to style his garden after the Japanese tradition."

The success of a garden in this style lies mainly with its authenticity, with the designer's close supervision of even minute details, and the rigorous exclusion of any conflicting garden style within its boundaries.

"Within its boundaries" can be loosely interpreted, for in the example on page 39 the boundary is an ill-defined line between the edge of the pool (a convenient dividing device) and the concrete surface of a thoroughly Western patio.

There cannot be, however, loose interpretations of what is Japanese. Each of these gardens is by a landscape architect, who has studied not only the plants that grow in Japanese gardens, but the deeper philosophical reasons for the

Tats Ishimoto design

The water on the facing page is all in the garden at left

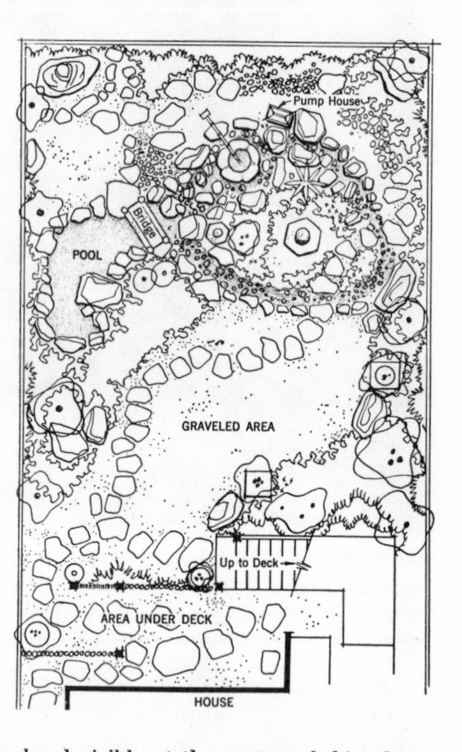

Importance of scale in design of Japanese gardens gets a textbook demonstration in this case. The garden is barely 25 feet deep; the bowl visible at the center of this photo is the beginning of the stream and pool system.

choice of those particular plants. Japanese ideas can be borrowed successfully by an amateur designer, but a full-fledged Japanese garden is in the province of the professional.

Fortunately for a Westerner who wants a garden in the Japanese concept, the climate of Japan is in some respects similar to the climate of the northwest Pacific Coast, the San Francisco Bay and Puget Sound areas, and the Monterey Peninsula among other coastal sections of California.

Water in a Japanese garden almost inevitably is contained in a pool that achieves most of its shape through studied use of rock. Many pools are suitable for fish, which are even more popular garden adjuncts in Japan than they are in this nation.

If the pools are not suitable for fish, they at least look as if they are.

This introduces the key point in adapting Japanese garden styles to American gardens: Scale governs all elements in the garden, an example perfectly set by the stream pictured on these pages. In truth, the water is seldom more than three inches deep and a foot wide, but plants and stones carefully chosen and placed leave the viewer to imagine the stream to any size that suits his mood of the moment.

Stones in this view loom large, but most would hardly strain a good college shot-putter. The view is from the bridge area and parallel to the rear of the house. It shows the bottom loop of the stream as shown in the sketch.

Stream at beginning, next to pump house, is only inches wide. Outlet pipe barely visible among stones.

View from bridge back to concrete bowl shows how small stream is. Shallow depression holds pool.

Lois Benedict design

Richard Tongg design

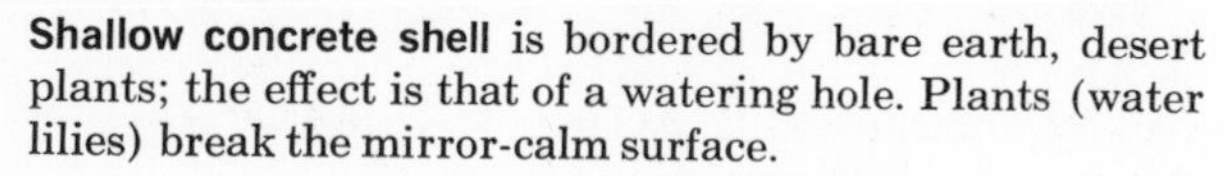

Shallow concrete shell is bordered by bare earth, desert plants; the effect is that of a watering hole. Plants (water lilies) break the mirror-calm surface.

Lacking usual ornaments, but a Japanese pool still, this example depends on stepping stone bridges, planting to create the illusion. Concrete shell hidden by grass.

These pools, like most of the other "natural" pools pictured, are free-form shells of reinforced concrete. The edges are hidden either with lush plant materials, or by artful use of large and small stones.

Shells should be at least four inches thick; six inches thick is better. If large rocks are to be placed on the floor of the shell, it might be useful to employ this trick: One owner broke his granite rocks with a sledge, carried the small pieces out into the pool one by one, where he reassembled the stone with cement slurry. The technique avoided rolling uneven stones across the floor of the pool, and so avoided the considerable possibility of breaking the concrete.

Another solution to the problem of wrestling with weighty boulders is firbrous rock, a plastic mass covered with granite chips and molded into an amazingly accurate replica of real stone. Sold at nurseries and garden supply centers, the stones come in many sizes. They weigh less than a fifth as much as real stone.

Free-form concrete can be stacked to a slope of about 45° with ordinary mix, and can be made steeper either with forms or with a "dry" mix.

If a form is used, the builder can employ the trick (used in the photo at right, above) of trowelling the top of the wall to a 45° slope. This makes it easier for plants to grow over the rim, hiding it. (Another method is to regularly brush a liquid fertilizer onto the exposed concrete of the rim, thus luring plants over it.)

A Japanese device which can be used to achieve a short length of vertical wall is a row of small-diameter oak limbs in a solid alignment. The butt ends of the wood are embedded in concrete to a depth of four inches or more, and a thin shell of concrete is then poured behind them

Mrs. John Jenkins design

Straight-sided concrete walls separate lush grass from lush field of water lilies. This type of pool can be made with technique described on page 27.

Sierra Madre Garden Club design

Gravel strewn up to the edges and on across the bottom of a free-form concrete shell can evoke the image of trapped tidal water on some northerly coast.

to form a watertight surface. (See photo, p. 35.)

Another point in designing Japanese or other natural pools: The shoreline should rise and fall in relationship to the surface of the water. Or, put another way, a few hills or hummocks should intrude to indicate that nature never creates precisely level brims for her pools.

Sometimes a concrete pool will be too permanent to fit the needs of a garden on its way to becoming something else. There are two ready alternatives. One of these is a kit offered by some pump manufacturers. A heavy-gauge sheet of plastic is included with a submersible pump; the plastic is spread, lined with sand, the pump placed in it, and the pool is ready to go. The other choice is reinforced fibreglass. The pools are prefabricated, or homeowners can buy the raw materials and make their own (a difficult task since the material tends to retain pinholes). The same material is used in fibreglass boats.

A woodland pond quite apart from either of the others shown on this page owes its character to dense undergrowth planting around a deciduous tree. Pump feeds falls.

Noble Hoggson design

Nagao Sakurai design

One shore is civilized; the other is rather wilder in this pool. The natural appearance of the stone on the far shore owes itself to the careful placement of each boulder in a balanced position. Further, the stones artfully hide a concrete stream bed. Woodland planting completes the scene. The near side is part of the patio area.

Native stone for natural pools

In the mountainous West, stone and water are naturally associated in the minds of most gardeners. The combination is everywhere at hand in streams and lakes.

Framing a garden pool with boulders is no easy way to do the job, but the results can be worth all the toil, sweat, and tears. In the intermountain West, a few landscape architects have succeeded in developing whole gardens around native stone.

• A man needs ample space for this kind of pool. Boulders fill up space quickly, and the shell of the pool itself has to be sizable to remain in scale with the stones.

• It is hard work for most men to move a boulder a foot in diameter. Most of these pools will require the professional services of a rockery man.

• Some types of stone—mainly the shales and other striated types—can be stacked in ways that look natural. Massive stones—the granites so common in Western mountains—look far less at home in stacks. For them, it is often necessary to create a mound of earth as a framework.

• Mortaring the interstices between stones, unless done with great skill, will be evident. In some gardens, this much sacrifice to convenience will be easily made. In others, it will be impossible. In the latter cases, the gardeners will need to resign themselves to a certain amount of soil washing into the water with each rain. (If the pool contains plants, soil will have to be in the water in the first place.)

Leon Frehner design

Leon Frehner design

Natural stone pool can take this shape in areas where shale or other striated rock formations are common.

In granite mountain areas, natural stone pools would reflect the tumbled quality of boulders.

• Rusty rocks can produce rusty water in time. The "rust" is ferrous oxide in the stone, and it will wash out into the pool when water runs over it.

In Utah, hard sandstone in buff, yellow, and pink hues produces vibrant gardens when used in combination with such native plants as cow parsnip, native juniper, chokecherry, river birch, and others. Locally available stones include limestone, granite, and a number of volcanic types.

In the Northwest, a preponderance of sombre-gray granite fits in with alpines, especially some of the dwarf conifers, and with subtle blooming flowers like rosy pink monkeyflower, penstemons, shooting star, rockcress, draba, and some dwarf varieties of dianthus.

Wherever native stone is going to play such a preponderant part as this in a garden, these observations by landscape architect Leon D. Frehner (of Salt Lake City, Utah) may be of use to the about-to-plunge homeowner:

"Rocks became important in my gardens because the mountains around us are made of them, and they are available in local quarries. They offer endless possibilities in design: for paving, retaining walls, waterfalls, and—for their interest—in ledges and outcroppings, or as individual pieces standing alone. I soon learned that each rock had a character of its own and was adapted to some special use. Sometimes an entire garden can be built around one or two interesting stones."

Frehner frequently uses this device to avoid ice damage to pools during fall and early winter freezes: Rock ledges, about two inches above the water, protrude four or five inches out over the water. This makes it difficult for ice to form at the walls. Even with this device, most pool-owners in hard-winter climates find it wise to drain their pools before the long freezing spells set in. The amount of water that seeps into a pool during thaws seldom amounts to enough to damage a concrete shell.

Lawrence Underhill design

Tiny scale exists in nature, too. In a setting of large boulders, two small basins recall a mountain spring. Basins are made of roughly cast concrete, filled with gravel.

Lawrence Underhill design

A similar pool to that at left, this one demonstrates clearly the need for a level "lip," if water is to flow satisfactorily from top to lower pool.

Natural waterfall designs

Small brooks on hurried flights downhill take the kind of tumble that looks fitting and proper in a "natural" garden located within a city or suburb.

Contrarily, veritable torrents whose origins are mysteriously placed midway up a property fence seldom appear credible. Credibility aside, such rushing torrents are expensive to produce, difficult to maintain, frequently in need of repair, and they can be most difficult to ignore in quarters that are cramped in any way.

As in the cases of Japanese gardens, a close attention to scale can make a tiny volume of water look much like a bustling small stream. Dwarf varieties of native plants can be transformed by an active imagination into their standard counterparts. Fist-sized broken stones can be arranged as if they weighed several hundred pounds apiece. Then, if the pump or standpipe is placed in a way that hides the water's source behind an outcropping of rock or some trees, the miniature scene can have an internal "reality" of its own.

In building the waterfall, the key is to achieve two pools on different levels, with a lip between them that causes the water to fall in a desired pattern, and to have the entire contrivance appear as if it had been there all along. These are some considerations in the task:

- The farther the water falls, the more force it generates. The results are picturesque, but they also create a tremendous scouring action on the floor of the pool beneath the falls. The floor of the pool should be made especially thick at this point to help absorb the wear. Also, a layer of gravel, or some other cushioning device might be used.
- Shallow pools of aerated water will tend to form algae. The sunnier the location of the pool, the faster the algae will form. Chlorine (household bleach or pool chlorine) is a handy solution in cases where the pool is without fish or plants, and it may even be used in cases where plants

border the pool closely providing that pool water does not splash continually over into the root zones of these plants. Algaecides are another effective solution in pools without fish or plant life in them.

• In nature, rocks lie in balance. To look natural in a garden, they must imitate that quality. This can be an annoying requirement to a man who has plenty of rocks, but none of the right shape. This sometimes becomes a matter of conscience.

• The face of the waterfall should be designed to be reasonably watertight. Otherwise, ground water will seep through its face, discoloring the water in the pool; also, water will seep under a concrete shell at a fast rate. It is especially important to guard against this in areas with cold winters, because forming ice can cause water-softened ground to heave enough to crack a concrete shell.

• Because waterfalls do tend to spill over, it is a wise precaution to prepare a firm bed of gravel when excavating for the pool's shell. This is the best guard against settling and heaving in the soil below.

(For a series of alternative pump and plumbing arrangements for waterfalls, see page 61.)

Michael Wills design

On a hillside, the builder needs only to follow the dictates of gravity to develop a natural stream.

Rugged stone of mountain desert zones stacked into a wall preserves its natural appearance, makes a fine backdrop for falling water. Stone is stacked dry.

Guy Greene design

Rock is unpredictable, and a small waterfall may occur wherever there is a boulder slow to wear away.

Leon Frehner design

John Caitlin design

A drainage problem gave rise to this stream at the foot of a steep bank. The surface flow could not be stopped, so it was channeled so attractively that the owners added a water line to keep the flow going when the rains ended.

Fashioning garden streams

Natural streams are every bit as various as any other thing in nature. A man about to attempt a stream in his garden will do well, however, to settle on a single model drawn from his own experience.

Mark Twain was able to pick great fault, in *Fenimore Cooper's Literary Offenses*, with a stream contrived entirely in Cooper's imagination:

"In the *Deerslayer* tale Cooper has a stream which is fifty feet wide where it flows out of a lake; it presently narrows to twenty as it meanders along for no given reason, and yet when a stream acts like that it ought to be required to explain itself. Fourteen pages later the width of the brook's outlet from the lake has suddenly shrunk thirty feet and become 'the narrowest part of the stream.' This shrinkage is not accounted for. The stream has bends in it, a sure indication that it has alluvial banks and cuts them, yet these bends are only thirty and fifty feet long. If Cooper had been a nice and punctilious observer he would have noticed that the bends were oftener nine hundred feet long than short of it."

Although Twain's primary aim must have been to embarrass Fenimore Cooper, he did leave a good lesson for future builders of garden streams. His criticisms are soundly based in observations of slow streams.

Water moving at a languid pace will wander through curves, always scouring the outside bank of the curve. This means that the stream

Mario Acevedo design

Islands symbolize peace and quiet. A concrete trough is the bed for a short, unnamed river that encircles the island of Patio. A recirculating pump hidden in rock cairn at upper right keeps water moving slowly. (Close view below.)

tends to grow wider at the mid-point of a curve, and shallower along the inside arc because silt will precipitate in the eddies of the curve. Stream bottoms tend to be fairly muddy.

A fast stream, on the other hand, rushes in a fairly straight line, detouring only where rocks bar its path. The rapidly moving water tends to keep such a stream bed scoured clean of mud. The bed will be rocky.

Examples of both are shown on these pages and the succeeding page.

The choice of one or the other may be governed entirely by the landscaping requirements of the site. Where there is a choice, there are factors that might be considered:

The circular course of the stream shown on page 49 makes for the simplest plumbing solution in cases where a recirculating pump is used

Hersaal L. Pitts design

Swimming pool pump is required to move the volume of water that rushes down this short, vigorous stream. Close study of natural rock formations produced stream so real it does not seem unlikely, springing out of a lawn.

to power the stream. A watertight rock wall separates the headwaters of the stream from its mouth (or lake). The pump is housed at the wall, and needs only lift water up a foot, in an almost straight line. Contrast this with the mountain-like stream shown on page 50. Its pump, located at the lower end, forces water back uphill through a long pipe to the stream's beginning.

Depending upon the designer's objective, one of three basic structural techniques will serve best. The stream shown on page 48 was originally designed to carry away surface runoff from a steep slope (the backyard became a bog after each rain). The results were so attractive that the owners "puddled" the stream bed with clay. This is an inexpensive way to achieve a stream bottom that is watertight enough for occasional use. It is also adapted to the culture of bog plants because a great deal of moisture is retained by the three-inch-thick layer of clay. The second stream courses through a shallow concrete shell designed to retain as much water as possible since it is a cooling device for the patio. This stream contains mosquito fish to control that pest. It has a standpipe and faucet located over the streambed, so replenishing evaporation loss is easy. Also, the same faucet can be used to fill the bed to overflowing, an easy way to water plants (and an easy way to lose fish if done carelessly). The third stream, located on a sidehill (p. 50), has a waterproof wall of rocks on the high side to keep rain runoff from carrying mud into the clean, granite bed (achieved by covering a thin shell of reinforced concrete with large and small river rock). This last stream also has a faucet hidden away in the rocks, since it loses a

Wayne L. Shira design

Otto Holmdahl design

Genuine streams cross but few gardens. The owners of those gardens are most fortunate if they can alter the beds of such streams in ways to produce the kinds of effects they desire, as in these examples.

good deal of water through splashing and evaporation.

The slope of any stream bed should be at least an inch for each four linear feet, if the water is to appear to be moving much. Gentler descents fail to generate much momentum in the typically short course of garden streams.

Natural streams in gardens

Building a waterfall on a natural stream involves engineering problems that will probably require professional skill. It is often necessary to build a dam to back water up high enough for a fall. By-pass pipes to absorb overflow during flood stage are regularly required on natural streams, too.

If the stream is used by spawning salmon, a homeowner is required by law to obtain permission from his state department of fish and game to dam it. In some cases, the homeowner will have to build a fish-ladder to compensate for changes that would block the passage of spawning fish, or keep newly hatched fish from swimming to the sea.

In redesigning the bed or course of a natural stream, great care should be taken to keep each changed factor in scale with the rest of the stream bed. Also, note should be taken of the scouring action of the stream where its course is changed. Currents will work against soft earth banks; in time they may chart a third course for the stream, to the great distress of the property owner. Flooding a pool to start a waterfall may bring the water level to a point at which it can exert force against a weak spot left unguarded.

Watson Clifford design

Simple, clean lines mark bridge of cast concrete. This one is large enough for two persons, but instructions in text at right can be scaled down to any size.

Sonoma stone makes ruggedly handsome bridge that fits well in a Japanese setting when large stones guard approaches. These pieces set in concrete footings.

Nagao Sakurai design

Ways to bridge pools

Many Japanese pools have small bridges, either ornamental or practical, across a narrow part. Woodland pools, real streams, and a few other sizable bodies of garden water benefit from the presences of bridges as well.

The three basic choices are quarried stone, cast concrete, and wood, in order from most expensive to least.

Quarried stone is a particularly Japanese material. One Japanese pool in San Diego's Sea World is spanned by a bridge hewn from a huge, single block of stone. It is a hang-the-expense solution to bridging. Narrower pools can be bridged by cut Sonoma stone at far less expense. The maximum clear span for this type of stone is in the three or four foot range; at least eight inches at each end should bear on solid surface, and ideally should be set in concrete footings as in the example at lower left.

Cast concrete can be used to bridge almost any gap providing it is adequately reinforced. The bridge shown upper left was cast atop a reinforced concrete beam six inches deep that runs the length of the bridge. In addition to the beam, the flat surface is reinforced laterally and along its length by ½-inch steel rods set in an 8-inch grid. The span shown is about eight feet, across a channel that connects two ponds. It is 42 inches wide.

The bridge was cast in place, using these steps. The beam was set, with concrete footings at each end. Then a plywood form was built, using the arch of the beam as a guide and with scaffold support for each sheet. The form met an excavation at each end that augmented the footing holes made for the beam ends. With the reinforcing rods in place, the concrete was poured in a continuous section. (A light scaffolding framework was rented to provide a temporary bridge and wheelbarrow track.)

The deck is three inches deep.

Wood is the commonest, least expensive, and lightest of these materials. In naturalistic surroundings, it looks at home more readily than either cut stone or concrete.

A bridge designed for use should be at least two feet wide, and three feet will promote a greater sense of security in he who makes the crossing.

Mario Corbett design

Curving beams are cut from 2 by 12-inch planks for this bridge, which rests free on concrete pads at each end.

Hayahiko Takase design

Glue-laminated beams can be bent to many whimsical shapes, to fit special conditions of terrain or design.

With this in mind, the main supports for a wooden bridge can approximate the following:

Two 2 by 6-inch pieces spaced 28 inches apart will safely span six feet; two 2 by 8-inch members will reach nine to 10 feet; two 2 by 10-inch members will reach 12 feet handily. The beams should be cross-braced at regular intervals; every two feet is stout enough. Scrap lumber can be used to make angle braces that fasten to beams and decking, or spacer plates that fill the space between beams solidly.

An arched bridge need not be a great deal more difficult to achieve than a flat one. It has the double merit of being somewhat stronger (arches are self-reinforcing) and more in the traditional line of bridge design.

The simplest method can produce only a slight arch, and it is to saw one edge of a 2 by 12 (or any other plank) into an arc. The narrowest remaining part of the plank should be as thick as the formula noted above requires. Tongue-and-groove decking can be nailed to the surface, or any 2-inch thick wood can be used in its place.

A more difficult, but more versatile approach is the glue-laminated beam. Using 1 by 2-inch or 1 by 3-inch lumber, bend one piece to the desired curve, and secure it firmly in place. Coat the bottom of the piece with glue, and bend a second strip into place, using a pair of nails each two feet. Continue to the desired thickness. Unglued nail-laminated beams are not well-suited to use around pools since they are prone to moisture seeping into the joints, thus subject to disease and insect penetration.

Snow-bent saplings form the beams and handrails for this rustic bridge across a small natural stream.

Thin lumber of this kind can even be bent into a double arc to connect two points on different levels.

A third solution suggested on this page is a pair of snow-bent saplings. The availability of matching snow-bent saplings is unpredictable at best. Forcing straight saplings into arcs is not an equal substitute since they will for a long time have a tendency toward catapulting. Where possible, the solution is most attractive.

Most wooden bridges over small garden ponds need not be anchored with footings. Stable bearing surfaces at each end will serve well enough, and will reduce the potential for wood rotting away in the concrete. All lumber used in this close connection with damp earth should be pressure-treated with a chemical sealer such as pentachlorophenol. Treated posts are available at many lumber dealers.

Roy Rydell

Village well is inspiration for design of fountain in patio at Sunset offices. Recirculating pump fills center well with water, which flows by gravity through pipes into lower basin, then over edge of wall to intake pipe where pump takes over again. Some steps of complex construction process shown on facing page.

Building and maintaining pools

A garden pool or fountain can call for a wide variety of skills on the part of its builder, who may have to wear the hats of carpenter, mason, plumber, tile-setter, electrician, and painter before he is done.

Even if he must serve a stint in each of these roles, a weekend home handyman should find himself equal to the tasks, because the pools or fountains that fit into home gardens would in most cases make good first exercises for new apprentices at each of these trades. Single purpose and small scale keep confusion at a minimum. No step need be hurried.

The following pages in this chapter deal with the nuts-and-bolts problems of design and construction, one-by-one, before ambling on to matters of maintenance.

The matter of masonry

The great majority of garden pools and fountains are made of concrete, or concrete in combination with bricks, concrete blocks, or natural stone.

Appearance, cost, or some other non-structural factor governs many choices of one material or another for pool walls (this book notes some of those factors on pages 18 through 31). For pool floors, concrete is used in almost all cases for the single, structural consideration that it is a solid sheet, thus far less likely to develop leaks than brick or other fitted-piece floors.

Working with concrete

Concrete holds a number of advantages over other materials used in pool construction. It is strong, can be cast in any shape, and can be reinforced with a minimum of fuss. It can be finished smoothly to minimize the difficulties of painting, water-sealing, or algae control. Concrete can be faced with tile, pebble, or glass mosaics to hide its basic utility of appearance.

On the debit side, concrete in volume requires a program for pouring, to avoid weak joints. It can be very heavy to work with. Except in cases where it is being poured as a shell in a shallow depression, concrete requires well-carpentered forms to make walls. Finally, concrete can be difficult to patch if cracks should appear at some date after the pool's completion.

Formulae: The old standard—1 (cement) • 2 (sand) • 3 (coarse aggregate)—serves best in most cases. Coarser mixes, 1•3•5 for example, do not produce the kind of watertight face that is desirable in a pool.

Experts recommend that five gallons of water be added to each "one-sack batch" of mix (1 sack of cement, 2½ cu. ft. of sand, 3½ cu. ft. of coarse aggregate). This assumes damp sand. An extra half-gallon of water with dry sand, or a half-gallon less with wet sand will produce a medium-stiff consistency. The mix should be stiff enough so that it will flow very slowly after being mounded with a shovel. Wall mixes can be slightly stiffer than floor mixes.

Sand should be kept free of any vegetable matter (leaves, wood chips) or loamy earth to avoid weak spots in floor or walls. Coarse aggregate should be no larger than 1½-inch mesh for the same reason.

Estimating amounts: Mixed in small batches, concrete will finally produce about two-thirds the volume of its dry parts. This occurs because the adding of water compacts the dry mix by about a third.

Five sacks of cement, 13 cu. ft. of sand, and 18 cu. ft. of aggregate will make about 25 cu. ft. of concrete (a 100 sq. ft. sheet 3 inches thick).

A pool 6 feet long, 3 feet wide, and 18 inches deep will require about that much concrete if floor and walls are uniformly six inches thick (and allowing for a small amount of waste).

Star-shaped inner form of closely fitted plywood; outer form of Sunset fountain is heavily-braced standard form of 1 by 6-inch walls, 2 by 4-inch main frame.

Workmen pour and tamp concrete in both parts of form, taking care to eliminate air holes around reinforcing.

Form stripped away, pool is ready to receive tiles and finish coat of cement, as shown on preceding page.

Mixing: The best solution for a pool of any considerable size is the rental of a half-bag cement mixing machine. The powered variety make relatively light work of this never-easy task. Amounts of only a few cubic feet can be mixed with a shovel on a board.

With the half-bag mixer, get ready half a sack of cement, a cubic foot of sand, and 1½ cubic feet of aggregate. Draw 2½ gallons of water in a bucket (mark it beforehand with daubs of paint).

Toss cement and sand into the mixer; let them blend until no streaks of brown or gray remain. Add the aggregate, and let turn until the pebbles are uniformly coated with the dust. Then pour the water in, and let the mix turn for three minutes, or until no dry spots remain.

Tip the mix into the forms (if so fortunate an event is possible) or into a wheelbarrow.

Hand-mixing on a board makes for a longer day, but for small amounts it is a practical method. The main requirements are a sheet of plywood and two shovels, plus the marked water bucket. The plywood should be free of holes, or water and cement will leak through, weakening the mix. One shovel is for mixing dry materials; the other is used to stir the wet mix.

Heap the mixings on the board a shovelful at a time, keeping in line with the overall proportions. When the ingredients are blended, form the mix into a volcano, and pour water into the cone. Use three quarts of water for each shovelful of cement in the batch. Scoop dry mix from the inside of the cone into the water, taking care not to break the dam.

On the first try, it does not hurt to go light on the water until the mix reaches a point where its final consistency appears to be too stiff. This will avoid too sloppy a batch.

Forms and pouring: In designing and building the forms for a garden pool, the idea is to come up with something that will produce a unified shell through one, continuous pour.

For a free-form pool, the forms may be nothing more than stakes to indicate the depth of the pour. For a more formal effort, the carpentry will be more extensive. In either case, reinforcing rods or wire need the builder's close attention if he is to avoid cracks in the pool later.

For a free-form pool that is to look as much as possible like a natural body of water, the steps are fairly simple, as described on page 36. A similar but somewhat more precise pool form can be achieved through the method shown on page 27. One good solution to a circular pool form is shown on the same page. It can be adapted to curved shapes of any kind.

For a standard, rectangular pool, there are two approaches. The above-grade pool uses the same forms used for any wall. A below-grade pool's forms might be simplified by the omission of the outer form if the soil is firm enough to stand without crumbling.

When full forms are used, the inner wall form should end at the finished depth of the floor. In most cases, builders suspend the inner wall from cross pieces of 2 by 4's nailed securely to the outer wall form supports. The inner wall forms merely hang until the floor is poured. Then, 2 x 4 or other scrap lumber pieces are set across each dimension of the pool and nailed to brace the inner form before the walls are poured. Nail short diagonal braces into corners for added insurance. (Sketches on the facing page.)

These general considerations apply to reinforcing, forms, and pouring techniques:

1) Any form should be coated with light oil, preferably a clean or fairly clean auto crankcase oil. This will keep the forms from sticking.

2) Use a flat-bladed shovel or some other tool to jog concrete inside the face of the form. This works gravel back from the face, making the wall smoother and more waterproof.

3) If walls are at right angles to the floor, take great pains to tamp the first layer of the wall pour thoroughly. Failure to do this may leave weakening pockets of air at corners, an invitation to later cracks and leakage.

4) For sunken pools, provide at least an inch of lip above grade level if muddy rainwater is not to flow into the water with each storm. This is a special concern if the pool has no drain system, since overflows are a potential hazard.

In the cases of natural pools, gravel-filled drain ditches around the circumference of the pool can solve the problem without disturbing the appearance of the shoreline. Typically, these will be 8 inches wide, 12 inches deep.

5) Before pouring begins, set up the cross-grid of reinforcing rods so that they are all about 2 inches from the soil. In the floor, the rods can be set up on stones, chunks of brick, or any other handy piece of rubble. For walls, simply drive the rods into the earth.

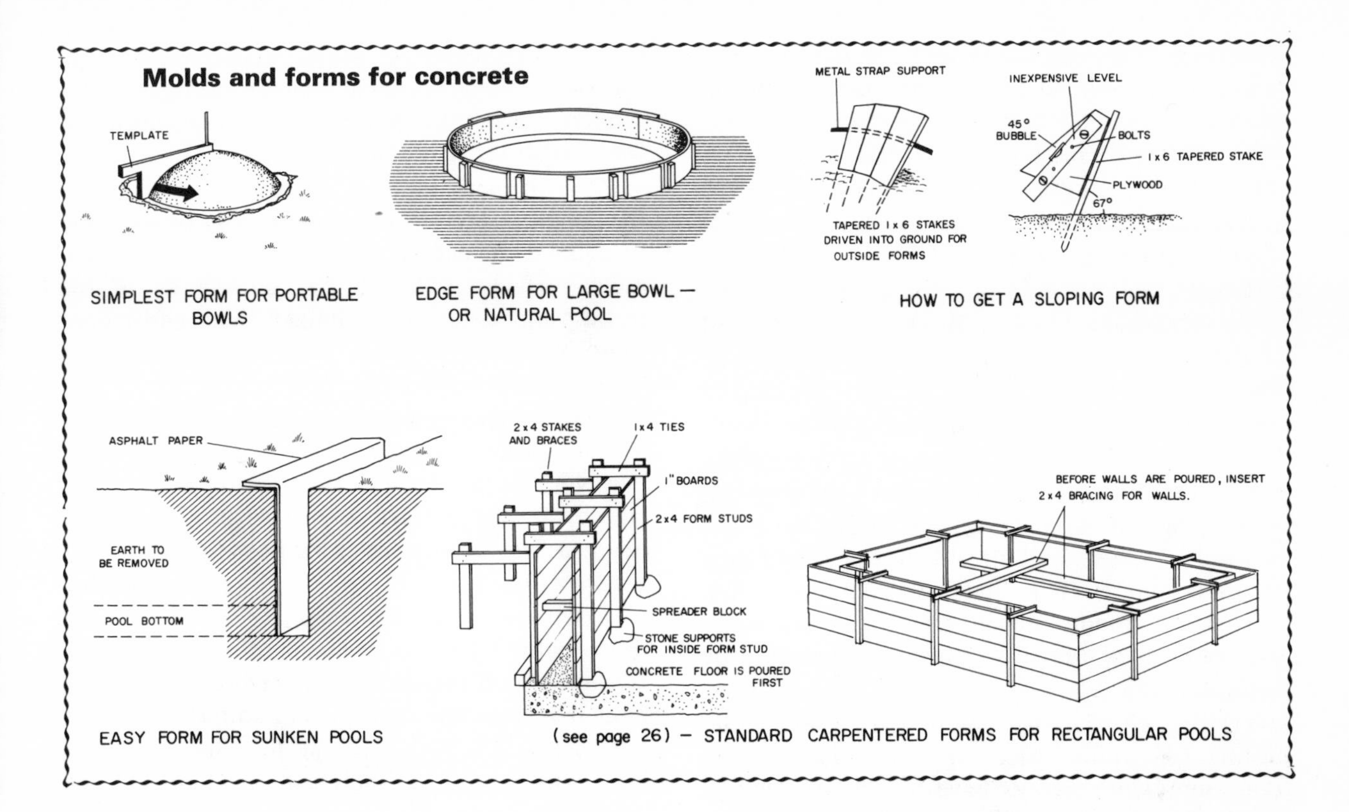

Through the course of the pour, check and recheck each section to make sure that concrete is worked down through the rods, and to make sure that the rods do not slip up or down from the desired level.

6) In pouring the walls, keep the pour progressing evenly all the way around the pool. Don't try to bring one section to full height before moving on to the next.

7) In excavating, make the excavation slope toward the drain rather than decreasing the thickness of the floor. Two inches is plenty of slope.

The first section of this book offers a number of detailed plans calling for "lightweight concrete." Most of them are for small decorative projects; they do not involve masses of concrete.

The term "lightweight" refers to the special use of porous gravels in place of the usual granite. The material is especially adapted to portable bowls and the like. It does not have enough strength for massive products, and is not at its best as a sunken shell.

Vermiculite is the lightest of these porous gravels. Haydite is both heavier and stronger. Two others that find frequent use are pumice and perlite.

Formulae: These vary with use. The lightest and weakest acceptable formula for vermiculite is 1 (cement) • 5 (aggregate), with no sand at all. A more usual ratio is 1 • 2 (sand) • 3.

For Haydite or pumice, a general formula is 1•2•3, and a very strong one is 4•1•2.

Each of the specific projects described within pages 10 through 19 has its own recommended formula.

Any lightweight concrete project should have metal reinforcing. Small-diameter bowls and the like need no more than ¼-inch mesh metal screen. Wide, shallow bowls generally require a combination of ¼- or ½-inch rods and metal screen, with the elements wired together.

Estimating volume: Lightweight concretes are rather less reliable than ordinary concrete. The best rule of thumb is to use double volume of dry parts; the addition of water compacts the mix by between a third and a half.

Mixing: A man about to crank out a lifetime supply of small bowls might use a cement mixer, but for many projects a mixing board will do nicely. The technique is exactly like that described for regular concrete, whichever method is used.

Forms and pouring: Because there is relatively little need for structural strength in the pools and fountains made with lightweight concrete, it can be handled in all manner of whimsical ways.

A number of methods are outlined briefly in the accompanying panel of forms and molds. Some specific projects using these same techniques are shown on pages 10, 11, and 18.

These general conditions apply:

1) Shovel wet mix into the form quickly, and spread it with as few trowel strokes as possible. The more the mix is worked, the greater chance it has of sagging and cracking as it dries.

2) When reinforcing, pour one layer half the thickness of the finished product, then imbed reinforcing rods or metal screen, taking care that metal does not extend into the outmost half inch of the perimeter. Then finish the pour, guarding against any sudden movement that would cause the reinforcing metal to stick up through the surface.

3) Mix all the dry ingredients well before adding any water, then add the water slowly. The mix should always have a stiff consistency for the type of project here in question.

How to make mosaics

Pebbles and shells go naturally with water, so what more appropriate use for them than in a garden pool? A decorative pattern not only brightens a pool, but shows the stones and shells at their best, for the water intensifies their colors while keeping surfaces clean.

Some craftsmen prefer to work out their designs first, as professionals do. But if children are involved in the project, or if the craftsman is attempting to achieve complete spontaneity, the pebbles can fall where they will with ofttimes delightful results.

In either case, work goes quickest and smoothest if pieces are first separated by size and color (and type if several materials are used).

The simplest way to embed the pebbles, glass, ceramic bits, or shells is to push them into the wet concrete soon after it is poured, but before it sets. This works well if there are only a few pieces to place. (If the entire bottom and the walls of the pool are to be covered, the concrete will set before the work can be completed.)

After the shells, rocks, or mosaic tiles are in place, let the concrete harden for three or four hours. Then carefully wash excess concrete off the faces of the decorative pieces, using a gentle stream of water from the garden hose and a soft wire brush, or a broom.

When a large number of pieces is to be used in a pool mosaic, the best method is to set them in a layer of mortar spread over the cured concrete surface. Although the process keeps the project unfinished for a longer time, and means more work, it at least has the advantage of water-proofing the pool thoroughly.

The concrete should be rough so there will be a good bond with the mortar. Work can be done, however, on a now-and-then basis; each patch of mortar can be left to dry without worrying about a firm bond developing between it and the next section.

First, wet down the concrete so it will not draw water from the mortar and cause it to dry too quickly. Then spread an inch-thick layer of mortar in a patch about a foot square.

Dip the decorative pieces in water (both to clean them and to wet them so they will not draw water from the mortar), then set them in place. As each foot-square patch is completed, spread another patch of mortar and continue. If the project is not finished in one day, mortar left over at the end of the day should be discarded before it sets. Start each new morn with a spanking fresh batch.

Experimentation is the only way to get the right mortar consistency. Consistency is of especial importance if the wall of the pool is being decorated. If it is too wet, the mortar will slide to the bottom, and if too dry, it will fail to hold the decorative pieces.

The usual recommendation is this: 1 part Portland cement, ½ part hydrated lime or lime putty, 4½ parts graded sand.

When the mortar has set, use a brush to clean off the faces of the pebbles, shells, glass bits, or whatever is used.

Working with brick

Brick will not bend to so many whims as concrete will. Any pool wall with so many mortar joints in it will almost certainly develop at least one leak. Brick is particularly susceptible to cracking in cold-winter areas. It is harder to

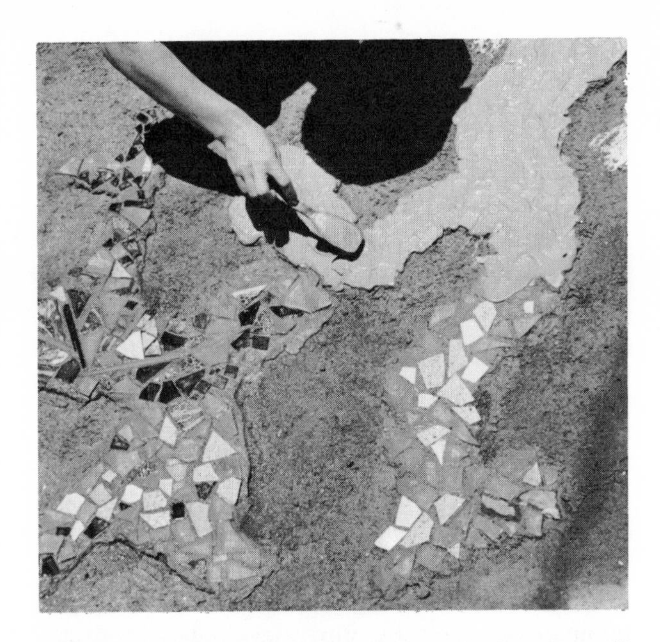

Mosaic in grout has advantage that it can be done in small sections if craftsman wishes to take that approach.

Finished work should look much like this: Individual pieces should make level floor; crevices should be minimal.

make waterproof than concrete, and tends to collect algae more readily because of its rough surfaces.

But for all of that, brick will never disappear from the garden because of its great advantages of warm color, inherent pattern, and traditional style. No adequate substitute for those qualities will ever exist in the minds of many garden owners.

A careful workman can make a sound wall of brick, one that will hold water in a pool for years. It takes excellently made mortar applied with precision, and it takes two coats of a good commercial waterseal to make a watertight wall.

A brick wall should be at least eight inches thick—the length of one brick. There are two ways to go about it: the wall can be two parallel rows of stretchers (bricks used lengthwise), or it can be some combination of stretchers and headers (bricks used sideways). The former method makes vertical reinforcing easier to manage since the rods can be mortared between the rows without disturbing any set pattern.

One way to simplify the problems of brick masonry is to make a thin concrete shell—three or four inches thick—and use it as the watertight interior face. A veneer of bricks on the outer face escapes any need to be leak-proof while producing the desired appearance.

Types of bricks: Bricks come in a wide range of colors, textures, and a narrower range of sizes. Size and color stand as matters of choice. Textures matter somewhat more in pool walls.

The standard brick measures 2½ by 3¾ by 8 inches. It is the optimum size for a one-hand lift, repeated 800 to 1,000 times a day. (This is the professional standard; a novice may find his arm gone rubbery a bit ahead of schedule.) The paver is larger, at 2½ x 4 x 8½ inches.

Of the many textures or compositions marketed, the non-porous faces of pavers and standard pressed bricks are more functional than the porous surfaces of wire-cut or similar bricks, since the solid surfaces take water-sealing compounds with greater grace, and resist algae somewhat better.

Estimating numbers: There is no absolute way to estimate the number of bricks a pool will require, because there are innumerable bonds, each of which will call for a different number of bricks.

The usual method is to decide on a bond, then work out arithmetically the number of bricks needed to make a section of the wall two feet long. Multiply that figure by the total number of similar units in the project and the resulting figure should be fairly accurate. In buying bricks, always get spares to cover losses through breakage or other causes. It is almost impossible to match colors between two different batches, even if both were manufactured by the same firm.

The least expensive bond is known as the rolok. See the sketch on page 26.

Mortar: Mortar is a mixture of cement, fine sand, and water, with a small amount of lime or lime putty added for plasticity.

There are dozens of mortar mixes, each with its school of supporters. Only four mixes are widely accepted among manufacturers. Of these, two are suitable for use in pools, types S and N.

Type S proportions are 1 part Portland cement, ½ part hydrated lime or lime putty, 4½ parts graded sand.

Type N proportions are 1 part Portland cement, 1 part hydrated lime or lime putty, 6 parts graded sand. (The designations M, S, N, and O are new standard symbols, replacing the earlier A-1, A-2, B, and C.)

Sand should be "sharp," made up of angular particles, free of dirt. When wet, squeezing it should not produce a slimy deposit in the hand; neither should the sand bind together. Special mortar mixes are sold at some dealers; others use a 50-50 mix of fine concrete sand and plaster sand.

Too much sand makes the mortar short. It will not hang to trowel or brick; smoothly tooled joints are hard to achieve.

Basic techniques for mortaring shown in sketches. Spread enough to cover four bricks at each time.

Almost any flat surface can be used for mixing mortar; a 2 by 2-foot square of plywood is as serviceable as any other sort. The following amounts (Type S) are sufficient for 50 bricks: 1 shovelful of cement, 4½ shovelfuls of sand, ½ shovelful of lime. Mix the ingredients thoroughly in their dry state with a hoe. Scoop out a hollow, add water, and mix carefully. Continue blending and adding water until the mortar slips cleanly off the blade of the hoe.

Never mix more than can be used in an hour. If the batch begins to stiffen towards the end, it can be freshened with a small amount of water.

Laying brick: Only a few tools are needed for simple bricklaying. These are a 10-inch trowel with pointed blade (for buttering mortar), a brick set (a cold chisel for cutting bricks), a hammer, a two-foot spirit level, a carpenter's square, and a stretch of fishing line.

Common bricks should be damp, but not wet, when they are laid. If too wet, they dilute the mortar and cause it to run, and they slip in the mortar bed. The stack should be soaked with a fine spray for about an hour and a half, starting at least four hours before the laying up is to begin.

Before starting to mortar bricks in place, on the pool floor string out the first course dry. This is a last check to insure the wall's ending at the same time the floor does. Leave ½-inch spaces for mortar joints.

A professional places a stack of bricks ahead of his finished work on the wall, and puts the mortar board behind him to the right. He reaches out with his trowel hand, scoops mortar onto the foundation (and each preceeding course to the one he is laying) to a distance of three or four bricks. With the trowel he furrows the mortar to push it out even with the edges of the bricks, then with his other hand, picks up a brick and butters one end with mortar. (Most men work along a wall from left to right). A quick tap of the dry end of the brick against the top of the wall seats the mortar. The brick is then placed exactly where it is to rest (pushing it or picking it up and relaying it is an invitation to leaks in a pool). Trim away excess mortar, and use that to butter the next brick.

It is best to build up corners first, then to work at the center section of a wall. Use a plumb level to keep in vertical alignment. Stretch fish line at each course to keep horizontal level.

Pumps and plumbing in pools

Plumbing and pumps for garden pools have been improved and simplified to the point where a weekend handyman can install them himself. A man who is too busy to do his own work can have a pump installed at comparatively modest cost. And, accordingly, maintenance requirements are minor once the pool is finished and the pump is working.

The mechanical heart of a fountain or waterfall, the pump, is merely a set of whirling blades through which the water passes and by which it is pressured into further motion. Motors are included with all pumps designed specifically for garden pools.

The greatest advantage of a pump over an ever-changing supply of tap water is that the same water is used over and over, which permits the growing of fish and plants, and at the same time aerates the water so that it stays fresh. (Most municipal water supplies contain chemicals that do not allow the growth of tiny organisms essential to fish and plants.)

If fish and plants are not included in the plans for a fountain, it is true that the cost of water in most communities is about equivalent to the cost of electricity for a pump producing a similar volume of moving water. In this case, the choice in great part revolves around the capacity of the garden to take care of overflow. Sometimes it can be easy to tie into an existing drain system. Sometimes the garden can use a steady supply of water to grow moisture-loving plants.

But, assuming the choice of a pump, the homeowner can select from a range of sizes, types, and prices to meet almost any demand.

Fully submersible pumps range from tiny 1/55 horsepower models, which move 135 gallons of water an hour to a height of two feet, up to a husky unit which will lift 675 gallons of water an hour to a height of 12 feet. The costs range from about $20 to slightly less than $60.

These pumps simplify plumbing to the extreme. They sit on the floor of the pool, and are hidden only by the water itself. Flexible tubing carries water to the fountainhead or to the source for a waterfall. Fill and drain piping, if any, are separate. Some manufacturers market kits, which include a sheet of heavy-gauge polyethylene plastic. These sheets can be spread in a shallow depression, and covered with a thin layer of sand to make a temporary pool.

PUMP PERFORMANCE CHART							
	GALLONS PER HOUR PUMPED						
VERTICAL LIFT IN FEET	1	3	4	5	7	9	12
PUMP No. 1	180	139	122	95	18	—	—
PUMP No. 2	270	250	230	205	145	50	—
PUMP No. 3	670	650	640	627	575	524	445
PUMP No. 4	810	784	771	745	679	613	514

The motors of submersible pumps are housed in watertight domes, permanently sealed and containing a lubricating medium. They operate silently, an advantage over other types.

Other pumps, with the motors exposed to operate in the usual fashion, are available in either horizontal or vertical models. As their descriptive names indicate, one type pulls water along a level pipe from pool to pump, then pushes it upward. The other type sucks water up directly and keeps it going in the same direction. The vertical type is the more efficient, but it must rest in shallow water of the pool—usually two to four inches deep. This sometimes requires building a special arm of the pool which can be disguised by stones or some other device. The horizontal type can be placed anywhere outside a pool, and it is frequently the answer when water has a long road to go from pump to outlet, as is often the case with waterfalls or artificial streams.

Both of these types are sold in an even greater range of sizes than the fully submersible pumps. For especially large tasks, industrial sump pumps or swimming pool filter pumps can be substituted for the more usually used models.

Don't be misled by the low horsepower ratings of pumps. A one horsepower motor can lift about 350 pounds (45 gallons) of water at the rate of one foot per second. It could move a small lake in a short time, and is much larger than needed for the average garden pool.

However, it is often useful to get a pump that delivers a little more water than the situation demands. The flow of water can always be reduced by means of a jet, clamp, or pinched tip on the outlet pipe.

To give some idea of different pump performances: The portable fountain on page 14 has a 200 gph (1/50 hp) pump. The waterfall on page 47 has a 500 gph (1/10 hp) pump. The waterfall on page 5 has a 1,500 gph (½ hp) industrial sump pump. The cascading pool on page 33 uses a ½ hp swimming pool filter pump.

Some pumps are self-priming, but many are not and need to be installed in a flooded position to retain their prime. (Upon installation, before their first use, some self-priming pumps need to be primed by forcing water from a garden hose into the pump chamber.) Be sure to understand the manufacturer's directions before starting the pump, since running one dry can cause the motor to overheat and be damaged.

The electrical connection for a small recirculating pump can be as simple as plugging its waterproof cord into an existing outdoor outlet in the garden. The addition of indoor switches or other refinements will probably call for professional help. (See the section below on wiring and lighting.)

The 1/50 hp motor takes about 15 watts of electricity. The ⅓ hp uses about 270 watts. Most pumps advertised as suitable for garden pools use about 50 to 100 watts, so the pump itself can usually be added to an existing circuit without any fear of overloading it.

For the greatest efficiency, the pump should be installed to keep the distance it has to move the water as short as possible. The non-submersible types can be concealed with shrubbery, masonry, or carpentry as the overall design permits. (Be sure to allow some way to get to it for servicing.)

The reasons for this are simple enough. If the pump moves a gallon of water one foot, and that gallon is still in the pipe, then the next gallon to enter the pipe has to push its predecessor along, too. The more water still fighting back, the harder the pump has to work. The table on page 61 demonstrates the decreasing efficiency of several pumps as they lift the water higher and higher.

In using a horizontal pump, the designer might take into account the fact that these pumps push water up more efficiently than they pull it up.

Pipes and fittings for garden pool pumps should be of galvanized iron, brass, or plastic. Brass fittings can be used with galvanized iron pipe to make assembly and dis-assembly easier. For a very small pump, rubber tubing can be substituted for any pipe.

Pipe should be at least as large as the fitting on the pump calls for, since smaller pipe only increases the friction between itself and the water passing through. Where no jet effect is intended, a slightly larger pipe can increase the amount of water the pump will move.

The intake pipe leading from pool to a horizontal pump should have its open end about halfway between the bottom of the pool and the top of the water (or deeper) to avoid a whirlpool effect. The intake should not be close to sediment on the floor.

An elbow on the mouth facing down will stop the whirlpool effect if the intake cannot be placed deep enough otherwise. In a very shallow pool, with the intake in the floor, a shell placed over the mouth of the intake will stop the whirlpool effect.

If the water is to go through a spray head, intake pipe openings should be screened with fine copper to keep the spray head from plugging. Coarser screens will do for waterfalls. (This amount of copper should not hurt fish.) Fully submersible and vertical pumps usually come with a screen built into their intakes.

Non-submersible pumps mounted out of the water can be sound-insulated by inserting rubber mat or lengths of rubber hose between the mounting plate of the pump and the block on which it rests. To avoid potentially noisy rattle between intake pipe and pump, use a short length of radiator hose secured with hose clamps as a bridge between pipe and pump.

There follow some typical plumbing designs for a range of pools from a tiny portable one to a full-fledged stream with torrential waterfall.

A portable fountain such as the one shown in the 'A' sketch (photo on page 14) is pumped by a quiet 1/55 horsepower submersible pump. The pump is bolted to the bottom of a shallow pan of glass fiber-reinforced plastic, and has a short inlet that extends up through a hole cut in the pan. It simply draws water down and then returns it through a short hose. The little pump moves water efficiently when so little lift and such short piping are involved.

To drain and clean such a pool, tip the pan up to dump out the water. If the pool is indoors, slip a short length of hose over the fountain head and pump the water into a pail.

A large garden pool requires considerably more

Pump and plumbing systems for pools and fountains

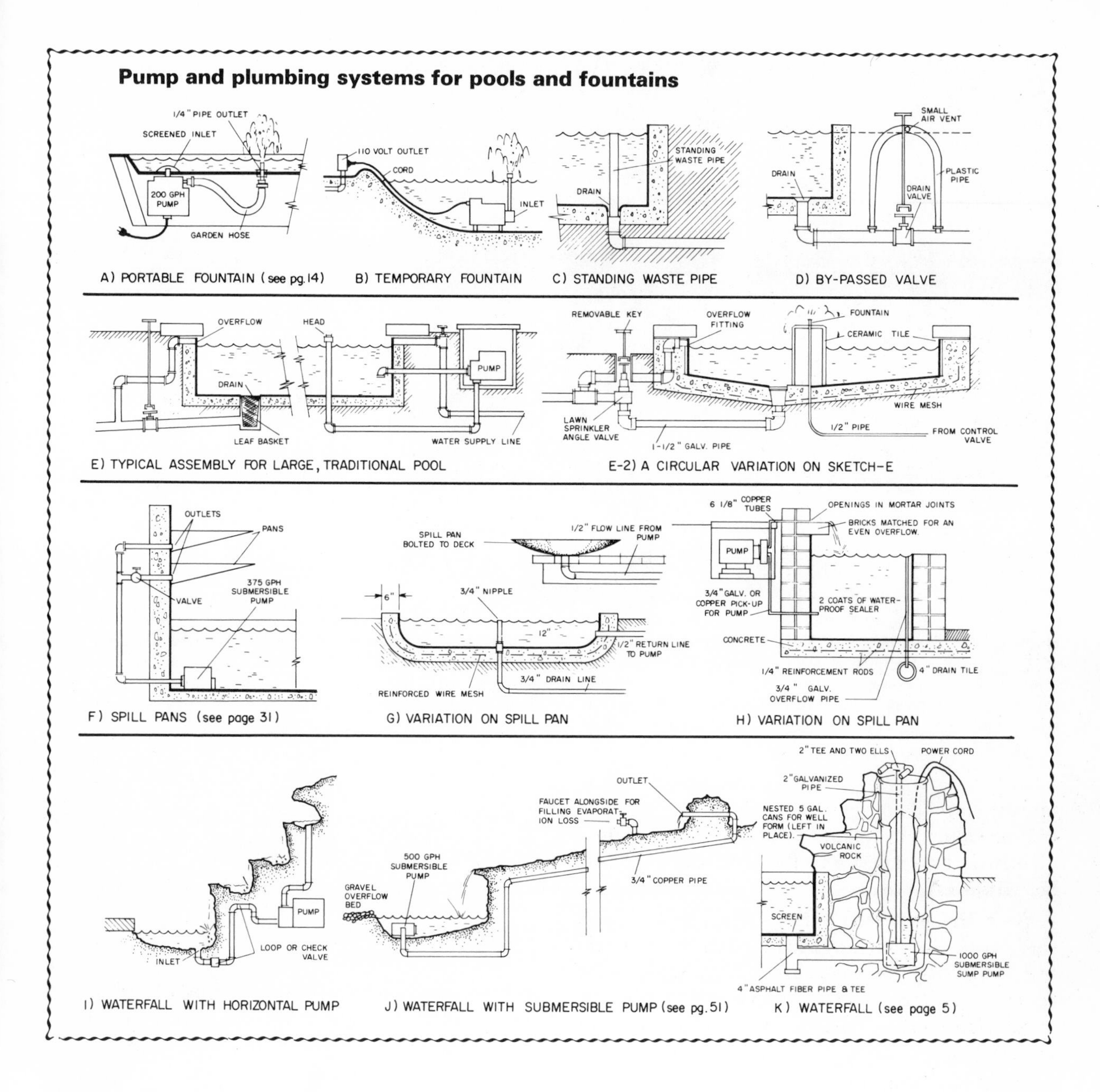

A) PORTABLE FOUNTAIN (see pg.14) B) TEMPORARY FOUNTAIN C) STANDING WASTE PIPE D) BY-PASSED VALVE

E) TYPICAL ASSEMBLY FOR LARGE, TRADITIONAL POOL E-2) A CIRCULAR VARIATION ON SKETCH-E

F) SPILL PANS (see page 31) G) VARIATION ON SPILL PAN H) VARIATION ON SPILL PAN

I) WATERFALL WITH HORIZONTAL PUMP J) WATERFALL WITH SUBMERSIBLE PUMP (see pg. 51) K) WATERFALL (see page 5)

plumbing to operate properly with low maintenance. Cross-section drawing 'B' shows a typical design. Here again, though, the plumbing is not complex and the water pressures involved are low (it is possible to use easily-assembled plastic tubing).

The pump for this type pool is usually housed below ground in a tight box. Placed lower than the water level of the pool, the pump never loses its prime. If the pump is large, with an open motor (common for large pools), the underground location also helps to muffle the noise. For any open motor, the pump box should be roomy and have holes in the lid for ventilation.

The pool's drain system includes an overflow drain to prevent rain water from flooding the pool. The supply line enters above the water, so the splashing is a reminder that it is turned on. For a pool of moderate size, eliminate the water supply line and fill with a hose, but a large pool takes a surprising length of time to fill this way.

Details of two other drain-overflow systems for garden pools are widely usable. These systems require only one outlet in the pool. Any overflow pours into the top of the standing waste pipe system ('C'); and to drain the pool, simply lift out the pipe. Brass pipes made for this use have a tapered end and a coupling to

Lawrence Halprin design

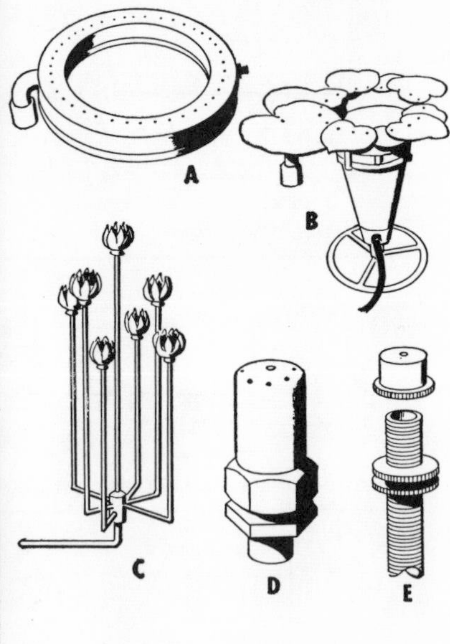

Fountainhead designs can produce extreme differences in the appearance of otherwise similar pools. At left, a large pipe with wide opening below surface. Center, pinched tip of spray jet. At right, sketches of specialty devices: A. Spray ring head with 48 jets; B. Bronze lily pad ring over pool light; C. Bronze water lilies, each with spray; D. Standard 10-jet small fountain head; and E. Spray head made of brass lamp parts (cap drilled for spray).

match; threaded pipe is used, too. Unless it can be hidden by plants or rocks, the standing pipe is quite obtrusive in the pool, since it must be within easy reach.

With the bypassed valve system ('D'), open the valve (located anywhere nearby) to drain the pool. With the valve closed, any excess water escapes over the loop of plastic pipe. Raise or lower this loop of pipe to adjust the height of the pool water.

Drain lines can lead to a sewer, to a dry well or sump, or, if the water is not treated with chlorine or an algaecide, simply out onto the lawn or garden. The pool outlet needs a screen or a basket trap. If the pool is apt to gather many leaves, the drain pipe should be large (3 or 4 inches in diameter) to reduce clogging.

To use the drain water on lawn or plants located at a higher level than the pool, install a two-way valve with a hose connection on the output side of the fountain pump, install its inlet at the lowest point in the pool, and drain by pumping the water out through a hose. This eliminates the main drain entirely, though the pool will still need a small overflow drain. Normally, however, one of the drain systems shown is less bothersome, drains faster, and avoids the risk of fouling the pump with debris.

Fountainhead designs

A man can achieve strikingly different fountain effects with different heads, and also by lowering a head slightly below the water surface. It is a good idea therefore, not to attach a fountain head so permanently that it cannot be changed.

Many fountain heads produce numerous fine sprays of water. These can be very attractive; they usually make little sound. Others, like the rotating head shown on page 29, throw large splashing droplets instead of spray.

Other heads simulate tulips, water lilies, other plants. Both the lily pad ring B and the fountain ring A shown in the drawing are of the type that can be placed atop a waterproof 110-volt light fixture. A light inside the ring of spray is very effective. The new low-voltage swimming pool lights work in a garden pool.

Several very inexpensive fountain heads can

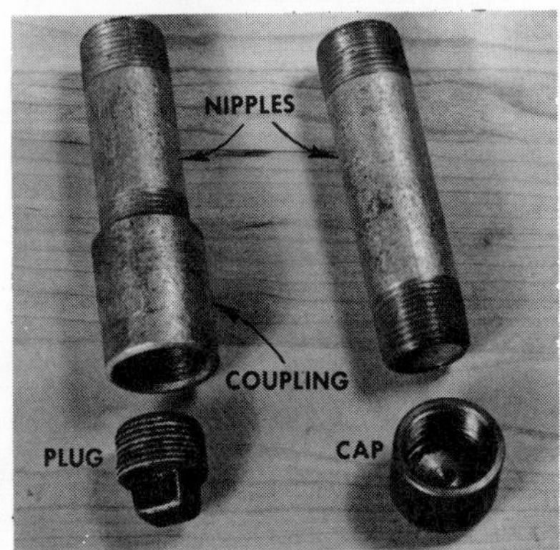

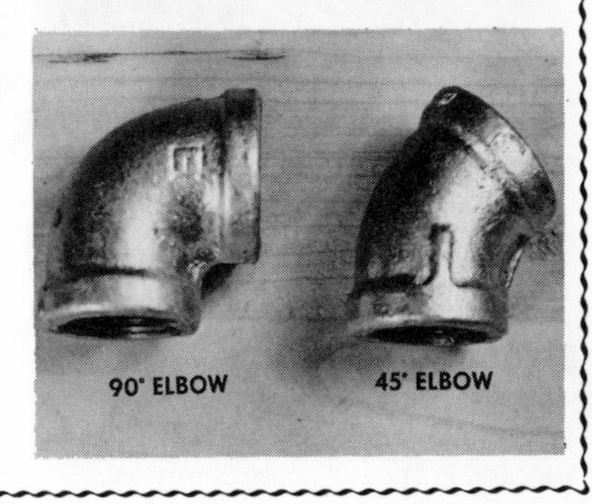

Common pipe fittings are shown in these photos. Top left, the union is used to join pipes separated by short gap. Top middle, tees allow pipe to tap into line (reducing tee allows small pipe into larger line). Top right, bushing joins pipe and fitting of unequal sizes while reducer joins pipes of unequal size. Lower left, plug and cap are two devices for sealing ends of lines. Lower middle photo is of several lengths of nipples, which are used to change direction in combination with elbows, shown at lower right. Coupling is another device to join pipe sections.

be made from the brass fittings made for the pipe conduits of table lamps. The brass ¼-inch pipe is threaded full length. Knurled brass lock nuts fit it, as do plain and decorative caps in which one can drill spray holes.

The fountain head of the portable pool (p. 14) is made of these fittings. A short section of the brass pipe is secured with two lock nuts to the pan of the pool. No cap is attached. The pipe is about ½ inch below the surface of the water. This produces a burbling fountain with maximum splash of the water and without a fine spray that a breeze could blow over the side of the 3-foot pool.

Pipefitter's primer

The addition of a pool, fountain, or waterfall to a garden often entails—as a matter of necessity or of convenience—the addition or extension of a cold water line.

A few simple tools, one or more lengths of standard galvanized iron pipe, some fittings, and a slight knowledge of plumbing are all the average homeowner needs to accomplish this relatively simple job.

If the pipe is bought cut to length and prethreaded, ready for assembly, the tools and materials needed are:

- Two pipe wrenches. One should be at least a 14-inch wrench. The other should be either a 12-inch or 14-inch wrench.
- A pair of wooden yardsticks, or a 6-foot folding rule.
- Pipe compound for water-proofing joints. A stiff brush for applying the compound.

Pipes and fittings: Galvanized iron pipe comes in a variety of sizes, indicated by the inside dimension. Most home jobs call for ¾-inch

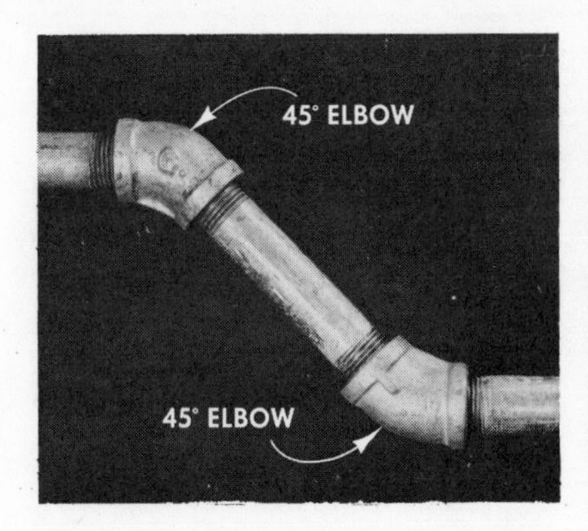

Two 45° elbows will produce a 45° jog in direction of pipe, sometimes useful for skirting obstructions.

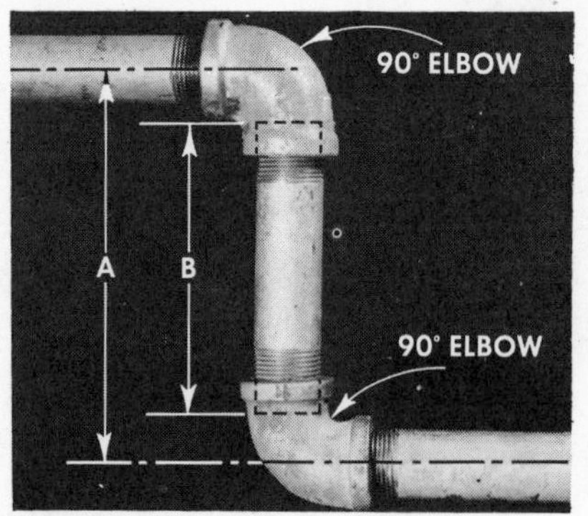

For right angle turns, subtract ¾-inch from desired length of pipe for each elbow used in pipe assembly.

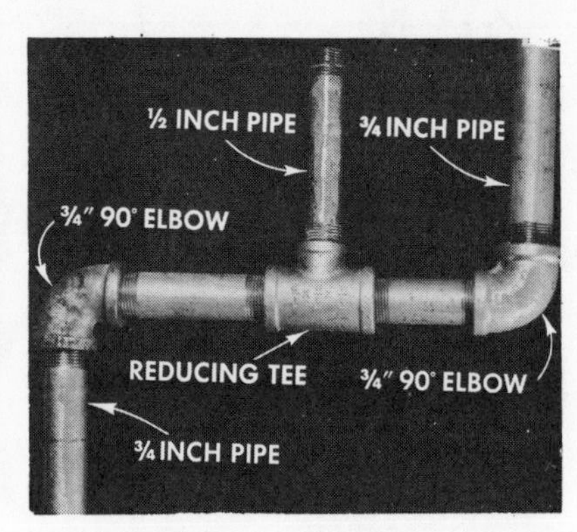

If pool requires smaller line only, a reducing tee can be used to tap off regular garden line like this.

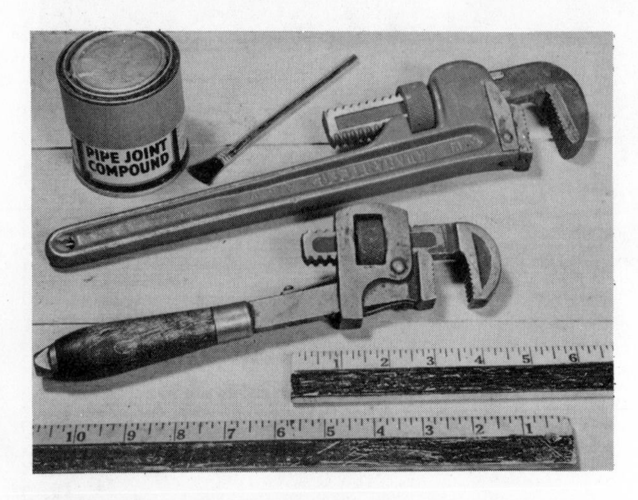

Pipe-fitting tools can be this simple if a man buys prethreaded pipe for his pool project.

When joining pipe, hold one rigid with one wrench, and tighten the joint with gentle pressure on other wrench.

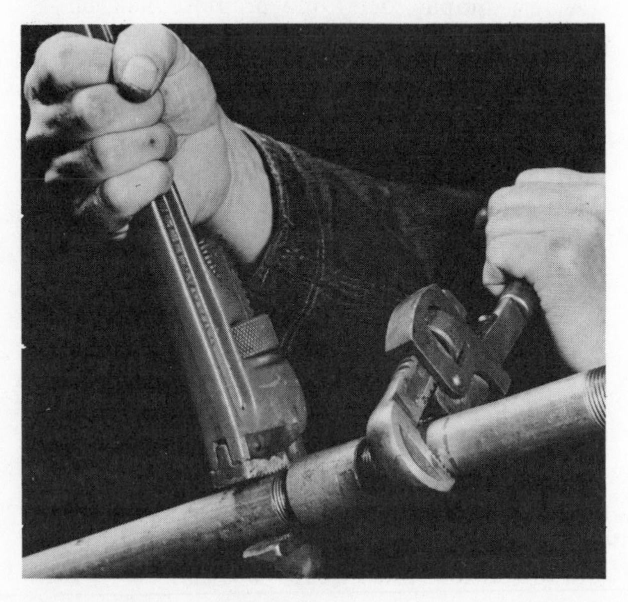

pipe (which has an outside dimension of 1-1/16 inches). However, if a ¾-inch line is already in the garden, a smaller ½-inch line leading from it may be enough for the pool or fountain.

Pipe fittings are used to join sections of pipe, to change the direction in which a pipe runs, to reduce or expand the pipe so that it can be joined to a different size pipe, or to plug the end of a pipe. The accompanying photographs show the commonest of these fittings.

Planning the installation: In adding a line, or in extending one, keep the number of fittings to a minimum. The fewer number of fittings, the fewer opportunities for leaks. To use a minimum amount of pipe, it is necessary only to keep the first lesson of high school geometry in mind: A straight line is the shortest distance connecting two points.

Assembling the pipe: With an old toothbrush, first brush out the threads of both pipe and fittings, inspecting them for damage or dirt.

Next, brush on a light coat of pipe compound to all outside threads, working it into the bottom of each thread groove. Apply pipe compound *only* to outside threads, never on the threads inside fittings.

Screw joints together by hand as far as they will go. Then, slowly and gently, tighten the joints with a wrench.

Too much force with the wrenches may strip off pipe threads in the fittings. On a good joint, one or two threads will usually show. (In joining unions, a large flat wrench works better than a pipe wrench. Both faces of the union should meet squarely.)

When joints are tight, wipe off excess compound, turn on the water, and inspect for leaks.

Using plastic pipe

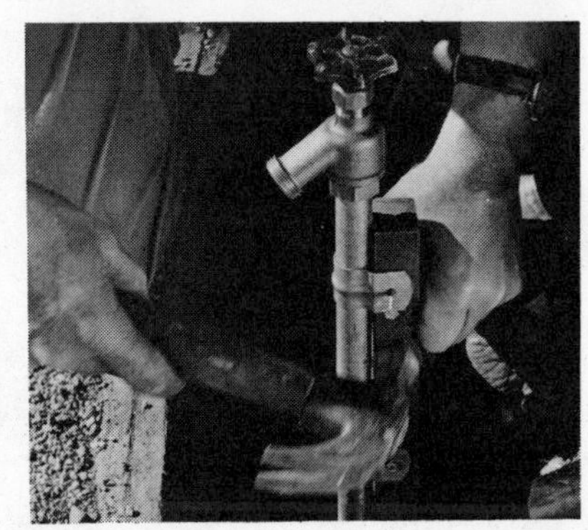

Installing plastic pipe involves these steps: 1. T-fitting added to existing plumbing supplies plastic pipe through plastic adapter. Pipe leads to new hose bib. 2. Faucet replaced on existing outlet. Plastic pipe to new bib covered by boards to protect from damage by tools. 3. Metal clamp holds pipe to plastic L attached to 15-inch galvanized standpipe and faucet at site of new bib. 4. Well-anchored stake supports the new standpipe with two metal straps. Final step is to backfill trench. NOTE: Plastic pipe is prohibited by some municipal codes.

A little further tightening may be necessary. If the leak is persistent, it may be stopped by wrapping a strip of tinfoil around the joint where the pipe joins the fitting, and tapping the tinfoil lightly into the joint with a hammer and screwdriver.

Plastic pipe: In some instances plastic pipe may serve in place of the traditional galvanized iron variety. It is quicker and easier to work with, and can be bent to get around corners; it is less expensive than iron pipe, too. On the negative side, it is less durable than iron pipe. Burrowing rodents sometimes will take a notion to chew on it.

If plastic pipe is the solution, choose a high quality polyvinyl chloride (P.V.C.) pipe or the equivalent. Never exceed the pressures recommended by the manufacturer.

Plastic pipe fittings can be joined directly to threaded pipe. Plastic pipe can be joined to galvanized iron fittings with the aid of adapters and small clamps.

The usual procedure for extending a cold water line to a new hose bib with plastic pipe is described in the accompanying series of photographs.

How fast will it fill?

One factor in deciding what kind of water supply a new pool should have is the rate of flow a water system will deliver, and thus the amount of time required to fill a pool.

A gallon equals 231 cubic inches. There are 1,728 cubic inches in a cubic foot, so for each cubic foot of pool there will be seven-and-a-half gallons of water.

There are three standard-size garden hoses.

A ⅜-inch hose delivers from six to seven gallons of water per minute.

The common ⅝-inch garden hose delivers from 13 to 14 gallons per minute.

A ¾-inch hose—the largest commonly sold—delivers about 20 gallons per minute.

Thus: A pool six feet long, four feet wide, and two feet deep (48 cubic feet) can contain 359 gallons of water. If it were filled through a ⅝-inch hose the process would take 25 to 35 minutes. Using a ¾-inch hose would trim the time to about 18 minutes.

Glen Hunt

Underwater fixture mounted directly beneath acrylic plastic sheet casts rippling shadow patterns on water's surface, the plastic, and the pool's walls.

Low-voltage fixtures attached to floating plastic lily pads illuminate pool floor and walls. Other fixtures alongside pool complete lighting scheme.

Robert McRae

Ways to light pools

Lighting gardens for night use is increasingly a part of outdoor living in the West. Garden pools in many instances offer a ready focal point for garden lighting designs. In cases where the pool is to have a pump, lights can be added at the time with little cost and great convenience.

When it is a matter of a permanent system, there are three basic approaches. One is submarine fixtures. Another is ground-level highlighting. The third choice is overall illumination of the pool and its surrounds. The first two of these choices can be realized with either standard 115-volt circuitry or a low-voltage system. Low-voltage systems are often less expensive than standard ones. A general illumination scheme is usually most satisfactory if it uses 115-volt circuitry.

For parties, any number of open-flame lights serve well. Luau torches cast dancing reflections across the surface of a pool, as do stubbier kerosene-fuelled auto flares. Something as simple as candles floating on the pool on pieces of wood may create the mood a party hostess seeks.

The accompanying photographs present some basic ideas for each of these general concepts.

Circuit capacities: The average household circuit is a 15-ampere, 115-volt circuit. To the user, this means that its capacity is about 1,500 watts.

A man who is curious to know if an existing circuit will handle more can quickly add up the present load; all light bulbs and electrical appliances have printed somewhere on them the watt power they require.

If the added power requirements of the pump and new lights still do not total 1,500 watts, no new circuit will be needed. Or, if the total amount of watts likely to be in use at one time is less than 1,500, the present circuit will do.

Most garden pool pumps use between 50 and 100 watts of power; most outdoor lamps are 150 watts. A six-lamp system of low-voltage lights uses only 150 watts when operating at capacity.

Choosing a system: Versatility in a system is sometimes an outright necessity, sometimes a handy convenience, sometimes no worry at all.

The main point is that the recirculating pump —where there is one—will require a grounded 115-volt outlet near the pool. Pumps come with

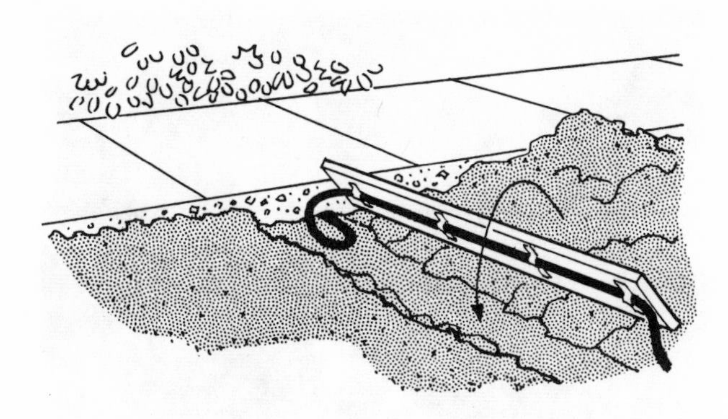

Underground cable can be protected by attaching it to undersides of 1 by 3-inch scrap lumber.

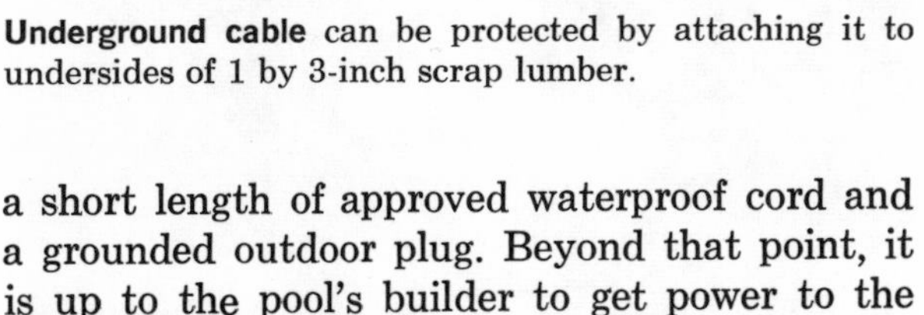

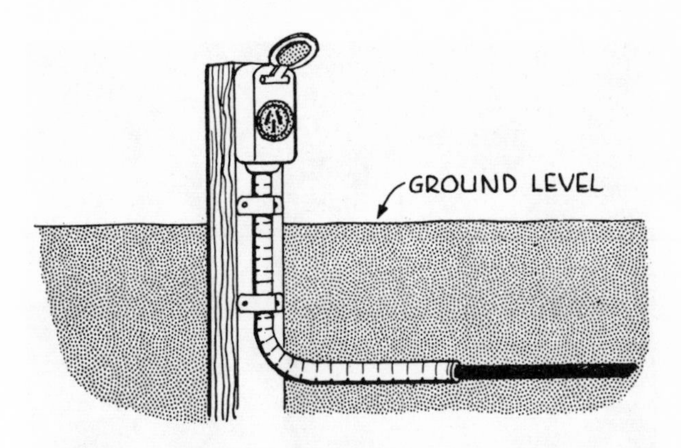

Outlets, other points where cable emerges from underground must be protected by some type of rigid support.

a short length of approved waterproof cord and a grounded outdoor plug. Beyond that point, it is up to the pool's builder to get power to the pump.

Regular outdoor lamps can be part of the same circuit used by a pump, requiring only a separate switch and the necessary additional feet of wiring. Extra outlets can be installed to operate any electric tool outdoors.

Low-voltage circuits can tap off a regular circuit at any point. The primary concern with one of these kits is the presence of a weatherproof housing for the transformer. The system cannot power any lamp or appliance except the lamps which come as part of the kit.

Adding a low-voltage system to some existing circuit is less costly than augmenting an existing circuit, and considerably less costly than wiring a new circuit into the service entry. If there is no need to add to the existing standard system, low voltage is the best bet. If it is necessary to add to the standard system, a man can stay with 115 volts all the way at about the same initial cost, but with higher operating costs.

Installing a circuit: All elements of an outdoor circuit should be purchased and installed with durability in mind. Municipal codes are unfailingly strict about the materials used. All outlets, switches, splice boxes, lamp sockets, and wires must be of approved weatherproof types. (Rainy days and damp nights are conducive to short circuiting in improperly sealed connections.)

Outdoor cable must be either the direct-burial lead or neoprene type, or be sheathed in rigid conduit when it is run underground. No. 14 cable is required on 15 ampere circuits with runs of 100 feet or less. No. 12 wire is used for longer runs or for circuits of higher amperage.

Either type of cable should be buried in a trench one shovel blade wide and 18 to 24 inches deep as a protection against accidental severing by some ground-breaking garden tool. If the trench must be shallower, the cable or conduit can be fastened with cable staples to the underside of 1 by 3-inch or 1 by 4-inch strips of redwood as a substitute protective device.

At any point where the cable leaves the ground, it must be protected either by rigid conduit or by flexible conduit secured to a wood post. In some instances the cable can be secured to a fence or screen post for this purpose, or to the pump housing.

Sometimes it is desirable or necessary to run cable overhead. Most municipal codes require that overhead cable be sheathed in rigid conduit if it is 8 feet or less above the ground. Higher runs can be left exposed if they are passed through strain insulators (like those on utility pole cross-arms) at intervals of 15 feet. If the cable follows the trunk of a tree, it is advisable to save wear and tear on the insulation by encasing the cable in thin-wall tubing.

A weekend handyman may be able to do himself much of the groundwork for a system of this type, but all terminal connections should be made by a licensed electrician. Most municipalities require that the system be inspected before any of its cables are covered. Call for an inspection as soon as the electrician is finished to avoid any later difficulties with code requirements.

In purchasing light fixtures for above-water installation, be sure to get weather-resistant materials (aluminum, brass, copper, stainless

Flicker of open flame is attractive reflected from water; these are automobile emergency flares.

Candles will float on a tranquil small pool; similar effect can be obtained by floating them in small dishes.

steel, hard-finish plastics, ceramic clays). For underwater installation—whether fixtures cast into the pool shell, or "floating" fixtures—use only UL-approved types. Underwater is no place to have short circuits. For ease of installation, choose and buy underwater fixtures before beginning construction of the pool. Some types must be cast in the concrete.

Low-voltage systems: The standard low-voltage kit contains 100 feet of plastic-covered cable and six lamp units, and a transformer. The transformer is built to handle six additional lamps on a total of 200 feet of cable. Simple connectors permit the setting up of spur lines, but the total distance is still only 200 feet overall.

The transformer is wired directly into a standard circuit. On the other side of the transformer, above-grade lamps are attached to the cable simply by slitting it and fitting the lamp housing onto the cable. The lamp housings that can be cast into pool shells, or that float free in the water, have short lead cables that attach to the main cable.

Main cables need be buried in as little as an inch or two of soil (nobody would be hurt by any short circuiting), but for their protection the cables can be attached with brackets to 1 by 3-inch lumber, after the fashion of standard circuits.

Curing and painting pools

Curing is necessary for a pool that is to support fish or plant life. Painting is necessary only to pools which need to be some color other than their natural color to satisfy the wishes of their owners.

"Curing" is the process of ridding new concrete of its supply of free lime, which is toxic to fish and plant life. The process is a simple one, and can be left to nature if the pool owner is in no hurry.

The accepted method is to fill the new pool with water, and let it sit for 24 hours. Drain, refill, and repeat three or four times. The last time, let the water stand for a week, then rinse the pool thoroughly. Refill it, and let tap water stand for 24 hours so any chemicals can dissipate. Then the pool will be safe for fish or plants.

Chemical solutions are marketed to speed this process for the man who has to get the job done more quickly.

Joseph Y. Yamada

Spotlight high above surface of water and aimed at angle brushes papyrus with light, causing reflection in pool.

Brick pools, and concrete pools which are to retain their natural color should be given two coats of a commercial waterproofing compound in cases where a sealing coat of 1 part cement, 1 part sand is not applied, or a mosaic is not used (this type of concrete, or the use of mortar is adequate sealing). The pool should be etched before a waterproofing compound is applied (see below).

There are several approaches to painting a pool. Metal tanks are best painted with an asphalt emulsion since it resists rust well, and adheres tenaciously to smooth surfaces. Paint of any kind may not be a sufficient protection for fish; new sheet metal cannot be sealed sufficiently to keep toxic elements out of the water. (Well weathered metal is neutral enough to support fish, so much-used laundry tubs are safe.)

Two kinds of paint can be used on fresh concrete with success, provided the surface is prepared. (If the pool is to contain fish, curing is advisable even if the pool is to be painted as well.) These paints are masonry latex and epoxy.

Latex should be applied with a brush or roller to a clean surface. Epoxy should be applied with a brush to a spotless surface. With epoxy, the key is preparation. One dealer says, "A flawlessly prepared surface will hold a coat of paint that will last for 10 years. It becomes almost an organic part of the concrete. A carelessly prepared surface will hold a coat that may last as many as 90 days."

Epoxy is much easier to apply on smooth surfaces than rough ones, mainly because the smooth surfaces are easier to clean thoroughly. Also, the paint's two elements harden quickly once mixed (two hours is the limit); brush work goes faster on smooth concrete than on rough.

The basic steps in preparing are the same for both types of paint. While the new concrete is still damp (but fully set), etch it with muriatic acid. Use commercial grade 32 per cent muriatic acid, obtainable from hardware and paint stores. Mix 1 part acid to 2 parts tap water in a bucket of enamelware, wood, stone, or plastic—never metal. A gallon of diluted acid will etch from 300 to 500 square feet of surface. Wearing galoshes, protective goggles (or glasses) and rubber gloves, use a long-handled brush to slosh the acid onto all surfaces. Scrub until the acid ceases to bubble, and the concrete attains a uniform, open-grained texture similar to that of fine sandpaper. Wash the acid off, and flush it thoroughly out of the pool (this is especially important to the man using epoxy). *Note:* Avoid flushing the acid into the root zones of plants. It will cause temporary burns to lawn and all roots of plants.

Paint is then brushed on, usually in two or three coats, according to its manufacturer's instructions.

When repainting a pool, all traces of old paint must be removed, unless the owner put that paint there himself and plans to use the same type again. After the old coat is removed, the surface must be etched, as described above, or the solvents in the new paint will soften the old coat and prevent a good bond.

Dealing with algae

The formation of algae in a pool is a natural thing, and a certain amount of it is inevitable in any pool stocked with fish and plants. However, algae does seem to get out of hand now and again.

Freshwater algae are any of several tiny aquatic plants, related to seaweed, which will coat a garden pool with scum if given time enough. There is no way to keep them from entering a pool; they can be killed or controlled.

Excessive sun seems to be the prime promoter of algae in garden pools. Since a minimum of four hours a day of sun is essential to the health of fish and plants, and more sun than that is desirable, algae start out with good competitive position.

The nature of the pool itself will make some difference. Sloping walls are an aid to algae because they expose more host surface to sun rays than do vertical walls. Rough textures are also helpful to algae colonies, which find them easier to cling to than smooth surfaces; walls with mortar joints and mosaic-covered walls especially offer the kinds of narrow fissures algae seek out. Fountains and waterfalls which send aerated water cascading in thin sheets across sunlit surfaces also promote the growth of algae.

Algae will flourish in alkaline water (found in most Western areas), so fresh water often only aids the enemy.

In a pool without plants or fish, control is a simple matter. Water can be kept crystal clear with liquid chlorine (household bleach or the kind used in swimming pools, available in several bottle sizes), copper sulfate, or algaecides.

Pools with fish and plants—or either—need greater care. If a natural balance can be struck, algae will not grow too thick; fish, plants, and algae will act in concert to the reciprocal benefit of all. Too many fish or too few plants will in time produce too many algae. Uncleaned pools are especially hospitable, because dead plant matter produces bacteria, which produce nitrogen, which encourages algae. Regular thinning of pool plants will minimize this. For quicker results than a natural balancing act, a chemical assault can be made. Fish breeders and nurseries dealing in aquatic plants sell several chemical preparations that work effectively. Scavenger snails may help if they do not become more interested in eating plants instead of algae. Potassium permanganate, recommended by professional fish breeders as an excellent tonic, is dangerous unless used in exact accordance with manufacturer's instructions.

Keeping fish in a pool

Fish—notably goldfish—can be kept with success in any non-toxic pool large enough or favorably located enough to resist sudden, extreme variations in water temperature.

A laundry tub or a half barrel sunk in the ground is about as small a pool as will support fish life out of doors. The same size container left above-grade is not big enough in any but a few special cases where water temperatures can be held fairly constant by some artificial means.

Goldfish come to mind automatically at the mention of fish pools in a garden because they are readily available, because they are showy fish, and because they are sturdy fellows.

These small members of the carp family have been bred for hundreds of years as hobby fish, with the result that there are almost as many varieties of goldfish as there are of dogs. The most unusual of these tend to be too delicate for outdoor pools, although they will survive in mild-winter areas.

Varieties most dealers recommend for outdoor use are: Common, Comet, Calico, fantail, moor, and Shubunkin.

Goldfish live comfortably in water ranging from 50 to 80°, and prefer the narrower range from 60 to 70°. They can endure a winter under ice, but will eat very little, and will not grow during the cold winter months. Where possible, it is beneficial to cover the pool with boards topped with a layer of straw. This will prevent the formation of ice. If the cold season is prolonged, one of the boards should be lifted for a short time during the warm part of at least one day a week to allow the fish some light. The cover must not be airtight.

Another trick that prevents the formation of ice up to a point is the use of an over-hanging lip on the pool. The lip should be about an inch to two inches above the water's surface, and should extend at least four inches out from the edge of the pool.

Never use a stick to break the ice that has formed on a pool. The probable result is concussion and shock for every fish in the pool.

Other sources of shock for fish are: heavy stones being dropped into the pool, and throwing the fish back into the water after they have been removed while the pool is being cleaned.

In a pool stocked with plants, goldfish will get almost enough to eat from natural food supplies of insects, insect eggs, and larvae. Supplementary diets of prepared fish foods should be used very sparingly.

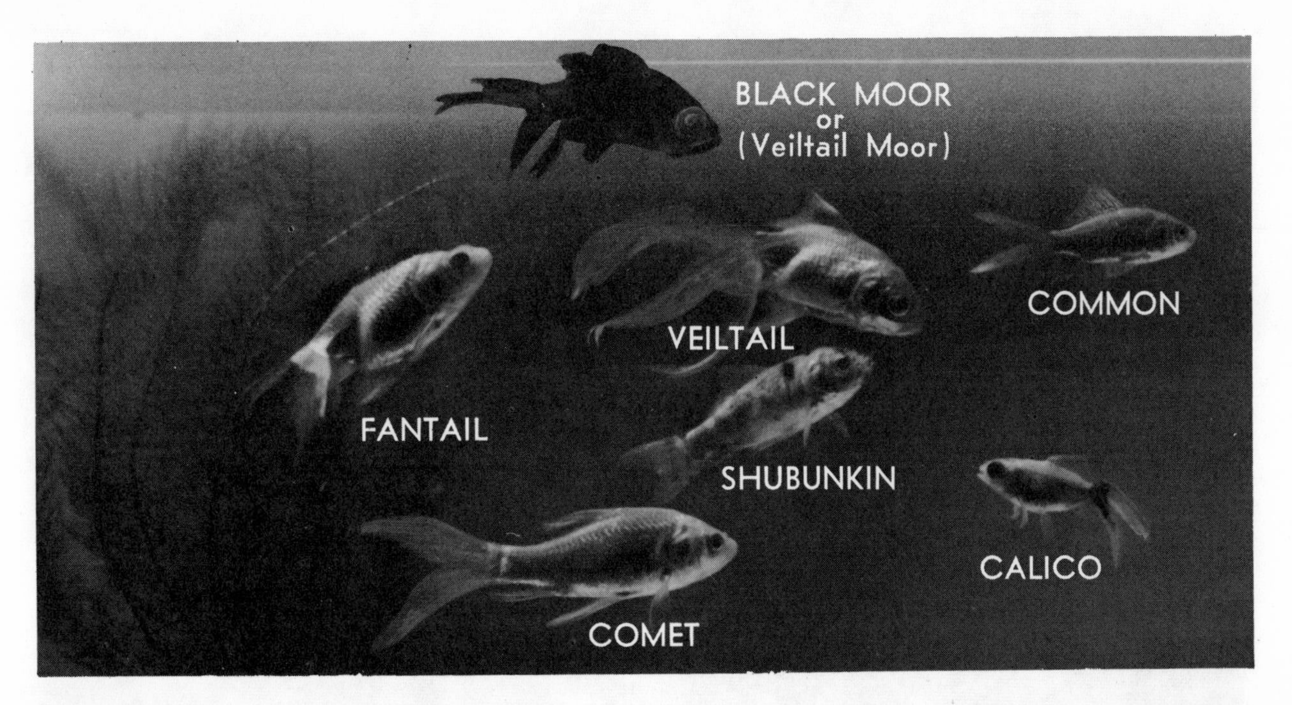

Goldfish are most popular fish for garden pools. In this photo are shown some of those commonly used outdoors. In cold-winter areas, the veiltail may not survive as handily as the other varieties, but it is fairly durable.

Each time a pool is cleaned, the natural food supply of the fish is disturbed, sometimes to the point of extinction. At the same time, new water can have bad effects of its own because of its chemical composition. Dealers generally recommend that, when a pool is being cleaned, the fish be put in a wide-mouth container full of water from their pool, and kept in that in a cool spot for the two or three days required to clean the pool and to "age" the new water. The aging process can be hurried with prepared solutions obtainable from dealers.

At the end of the process the fish are returned to the pool by submerging their temporary container in the pool almost to its rim, so water temperatures of the two bodies can equalize slowly. After two or three hours, the temporary container is fully submerged and tipped so the fish can swim out into the main pool.

Their feeding of prepared foods can be augmented slightly for a week or two while a natural food supply builds again. A small amount of prepared meal once a day is enough. A "small" amount is as much as the fish will eat in five or ten minutes.

Goldfish will keep a pool clean of mosquito larvae. A tougher fish which will serve the same purpose is *gambusia affinis*, the mosquito fish, which can be obtained free in areas served by mosquito control boards. The fish is nowhere near as showy as goldfish, but it will endure in less favorable conditions. It is not commonly sold by dealers because it is not popular with hobbyists; the state of California, Arizona, and Utah maintain mosquito control boards.

Almost any man who has spent considerable time in fruitless quest of gamefish can be led to think highly of stocking a private pool with trout or bass.

It is very difficult to stock trout in private pools because they need highly aerated water ranging in temperature from 48 to 65°, never warmer. This is a most difficult state to achieve in a small body of water. Few have succeeded at it without going to unreasonable cost.

Largemouth bass, on the other hand, can be raised in a small pool with success. This fish likes warm water—up to 80°, and will survive under ice. Some state fish and game departments will provide bass to private pool owners after they have inspected the pool and found it satisfactory. (The inspection can be of plans.) Interested persons should contact their state fish and game department in advance of planning their pool to find out what is required.

Authorities recommend a mixed planting of bass and bluegills; bass forage on the smaller fish.

Edith Campbell

Any number of moods can be created by the kind of plants used around a pool. Here a natural, serene appearance is attained by the use of weeping *Pittosporum phillyraeoides* behind the garden pool, flanked with low juniper. Around the rim of the pool a carpet of helxine makes a soft edging. Lily pads drift on the pool's surface.

Plants in and around the pool

A well-designed pool, properly planted is rewardingly trouble-free. There is no weeding, cultivating, watering, and almost no pest control. Yet its few feet of surface can produce the kind of rare, fragile beauty associated with the tropical greenhouse.

Specifically there are five new environments a pool brings to a garden. Each makes definite requirements for the type of plants that will grow there.

(1) Just beyond the pool's concrete sides, where the soil is subject to seepage. Good for moisture lovers like water iris, elephant ears, horsetail.

(2) Around the pool's shoreline. All the above plus water poppy, water canna, Egyptian paper plant, and creeping primrose are at home.

(3) Under the surface, where plants are submerged, leaves and all. Recommended plants include water Hawthorn, arrowhead, elodea, valisneria.

(4) Floating on the surface. Such aquatics as water hyacinth, tiny azolla, and duck weed are prime considerations.

(5) Roots in bottom, leaves on top. Most popular here are hardy and tropical water lilies.

One word of caution: Chlorine has become associated with pool cleanliness. But chlorine should never be used when there is life in a pool—either fish or plants.

Plants around the pool

Border plants thrive on the moist soil around the pool, providing a handsome backdrop for the plants in the pool. Possible bog species include the following:

Baby's tears—*(Helxine soleirolii)*. Creeping moss-like perennial herb with tiny white flowers makes cool, luxuriant ground cover near pools. Use it where it won't be stepped on, in shade.

Primrose willow—*(Jussiaea repens)*. A vine for pool's edge. Needs 1 inch of water or very soggy soil. Produces waxy green leaves and tall, primrose-like yellow flowers.

Elephants-Ear — *(Colocasia esculenta)*. Very showy plant of medium height gives garden a tropical look. Needs shade or partial shade. Spreads by root division.

Egyptian paper plant — *(Cyperus papyrus)*. Will grow to 10 feet but can be kept pruned to 5 feet. Noted for foot long tufts of thread-like flower stalks at tops of reedlike stems. Root in several inches of water and plant in sun.

Giant Arrowhead — *(Sagittaria sagittifolia)*. From dark green arrow-shaped leaves emerge spike-like clusters of white flowers. Grows 1 to 4 feet, spreads by runners. Thin occasionally.

Horsetail— *(Equisetum hyemale)*. One of the most popular pool plants, this vigorous grower is best controlled in a container whether planted in or near the pool. Bright green jointed stems give vertical accent. Needs afternoon shade.

Plantain lily — *(Hosta plantaginea)*. Large, shiny, heart-shaped leaves and white, scented flowers. Ideal at shallow edge of pool. Spreads rapidly. Propagate by root division.

Umbrella plant — *(Cyperus alternifolius)*. A relative of the Egyptian paper plant it thrives in shallow water or moist ground achieving a height of 2 feet. Propagate by division or seeds.

Water canna— *(Thalia)*. Deep purple flowers on long arching stems distinguish this perennial herb. Bold, spear-shaped foliage. Flourishes in an inch or two of water.

Water iris—*(Iris versicolor)*. Sought after for their color (blue-purple) and their dense foliage. Blooms late spring. Needs moisture.

Water poppy — *(Hydrocleys nymphoides)*. Miniature yellow flowers bloom best when plant is in 1 to 3 inches of water. Discussed with water lilies.

Bettler Baldwin-Owen Peters design

Growing in pots set on corner of pool floor are horsetail and papyrus. Shallow clay pots filled with succulents sit securely on a wide tile-surfaced wall along pool.

Horsetail planted in a concrete box constructed with 4-inch sides and 9 inches deep, gets all the moisture it needs, yet it never becomes a nuisance to owner.

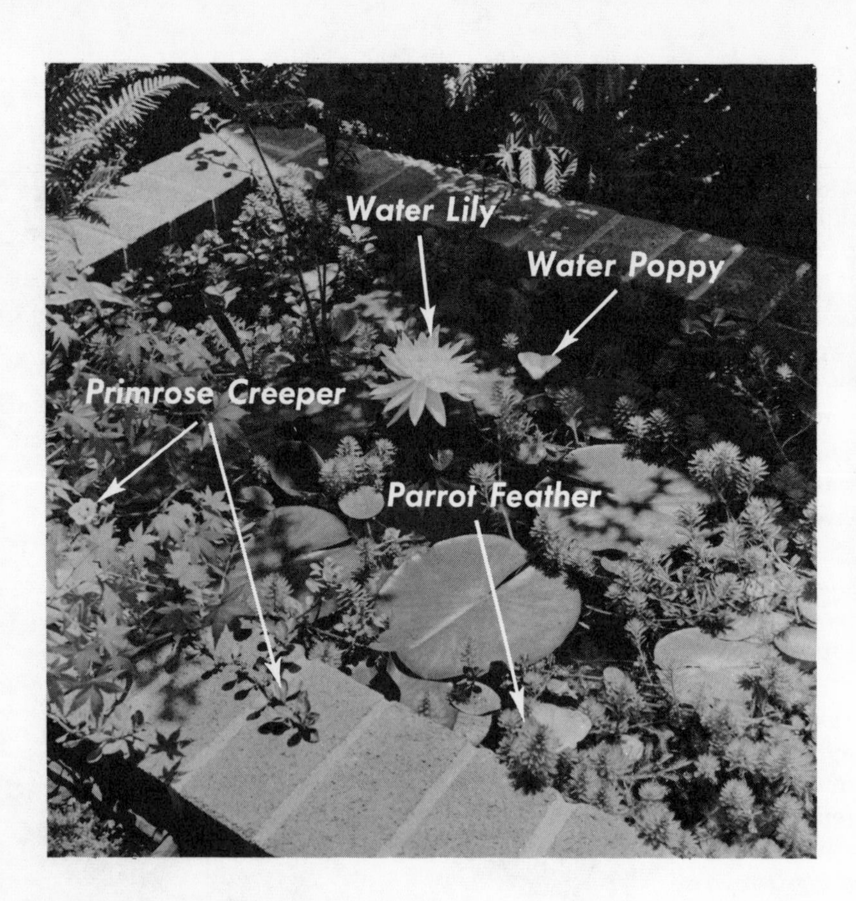

Gay, willing water poppies resemble California poppies, are a substitute for lilies in shallow, small pools.

At left, ferns shade one corner of pool. Primrose creeper in shallow water softens the edge of the pool.

Plants in the pool

Water lilies are easily the favorites of most water gardeners. There are, however, a number of other plants available for inclusion in a pool garden. If you have goldfish in your pool submerged oxygenating plants are a necessity as they supply oxygen to the water. They also keep the water clear and provide spawning places for the fish.

In small shallow pools that are less than two feet in depth it is possible to plant directly into soil that has been placed at the bottom of the pool. Most water gardeners will enjoy the versatility afforded them when they choose to plant in movable boxes. This will mean easy access to the bottom of the pool which facilitates cleaning and allows better control over the growth and spreading of the plants in the pool.

Arrowhead — *(Sagittaria graminea)*. Belongs to the same genus as the arrowhead mentioned for around the pool. But this one is used quite differently. It is primarily an oxygenator, growing freely in water, its grasslike leaves mainly submerged.

Azolla. Floats on water surface. This fast-growing mosslike plant is best used in small pools where it can be controlled. It is dark green in shade, turns red in sun.

Duckweed — *(Lemna minor)*. Tiny leaves cover a pool so rapidly this plant can easily be more of a nuisance than pool owners will put up with. One expert notes that fish eat its tender roots which act as a laxative and serve nicely as a fish tonic.

Elodea. Free-growing oxygenator needs sun. A perennial, it propagates by runner. Full, slender foliage grows under water. Pinch off old growth to control.

Lotus — *(Nelumbo)*. The East Indian lotus is one of those plants which looks difficult to grow but isn't. Thick, succulent stems rise from the rootstocks in spring, supporting the magnificent round leaves above the water surface about 5 or 6 feet. Flowers, often a foot across, are held above the leaves, and are single or double in pink, or white and red combinations.

Lotuses are hardy anywhere the rootstocks don't freeze. Lotus roots grow in circles so pamper them by using a round pool or tub. Start with 2 inches of manure as the bottom layer;

Given sun, plenty of room, and two summer feedings, water lilies will flower steadily from spring to fall.

Deep pink Rose Star is member of semi-hardy star lily group, tropical hybrids with long stems and heavy bloom.

Blue Triumph, a hybrid of native and tropical parents, survives outdoors all year in mild-winter areas.

cover with soil, allowing 8 inches of water above soil level. When planting rootstock, lay it horizontally in a shallow trench and cover with soil, letting the growing tip protrude above the soil. (For information on planting lotus in tubs or half-barrels, see page 80.)

Parrot's feather—*(Myriophyllum brasiliense)*. Light green feathery leaves drift on the surface of the water or float over the basin of a fountain. Provides good spawning area for fish.

Eel-grass — *(Valisneria)*. Long, ribbon-like leaves grow as high as two feet. Very good for oxygen.

Water hawthorn—*(Aponogeton distachyus)*. The big advantage of water hawthorn is its winter flowering habit, unique among the common aquatics. One grower in Southern California reports that during an especially cold winter, he found water hawthorn's little white flowers encased in ice. It needs 8 inches of water and a rich soil mix in a submerged pot or pond bottom. It has tuberous rootstocks and floating, rather narrow leaves.

Water hyacinth—*(Eichornia)*. There are two species of water hyacinth. One, *Eichornia crassipes,* was introduced into Florida streams and has now multiplied so profusely as to menace navigation. Nonetheless, when contained in a garden pool it is a valuable plant. It is a floating species, with inflated leafstalks and erect leaves. Flowers are violet with a yellow eye and are borne in clusters on erect spikes. The trick in growing them well is to prevent their drifting about with the wind, which seems to weaken them. A small frame will solve this problem; for directions see page 80.

Dangling roots of water hyacinths are ideal spawning territory for goldfish.

The choicer species of water hyacinth is *E. azurea.* It bears purplish-blue flowers with a peacock eye in the center. Unlike *E. crassipes* its stalks are not inflated, and it moors itself to the bottom like a water lily.

Water lettuce—*(Pistia Stratiotes)*. Comes by its name because of its resemblance to garden lettuce. It floats on the surface of the pool trailing long, hairlike roots. Water lettuce requires some sun and moisture but does fairly well in partial shade. It seems to do best when it is within reach of a fountain or spray of water. Roots should be allowed to take hold in a container of soil or reach a soil bottom. This enhances growth. Leaves have a blue-green color. The plant is also known as shell-flower.

Water lilies. Water lilies come in hundreds of shapes, varieties and colors but they divide sharply into two different classes: The hardy lilies, hybrids of temperate American and European wild forms; and the tropicals from Africa, Mexico and India. Each has its particular merits.

The hardy lilies are easy to grow and but little effort is rewarded with abundant and beautiful

Violet water hyacinth grows wild in Florida. Inflated, spongy stems keep it afloat on surface of the water.

Formosa, a pink flowered water lily, is rugged and easy to grow. It flowers in profusion all summer long.

Tall-growing lotus fits in background or pool center, as it isn't fussy about water depth. Fragrant flowers.

blooms. The tropicals make more demands but produce blooms larger in size and in color range. Almost all tropicals are fragrant.

In those areas of the Southwest that are safe for oranges, a few of the hardier tropical hybrids will survive through the winter. Elsewhere, all tropicals are treated as annuals, bought and planted in the spring, discarded in the fall. Attempts to winter roots in tubs indoors usually fail. Tropical lilies are shipped in wet excelsior, and cannot stand even a short dry-out. Plant them promptly in the mucky soil of the pool bottom or in a planting box after the pool is filled and ready for them.

Hardy kinds, on the other hand, are extremely easy to grow. They die back with the first frost, winter safely, even under ice, and come back anew each spring. Rootstock may be planted in dry soil and the pool filled afterwards.

A pool for water lilies should be two feet deep. They need about a foot of rich soil for their hungry roots and a foot of water above them. They will grow extremely well in the soil filled bottom of the pool, but it's much easier to care for them in planting boxes. One reason is that such water weeds as nitella and pondweed, which thrive during the winter when water lilies are dormant, are apt to invade the bottom soil and choke the lilies out. Also, box culture means a cleaner pool.

Water lilies are voracious feeders. They want plenty of surface area for leaves, which are produced continuously through summer. In large pools allow about 25 square feet per plant, if possible. Side dressings—one in June, one in July—mean more leaves, more flowers. Make heavy paper or cloth pouches, something like tea bags, put a teaspoon of balanced fertilizer in each, then poke about three of the bags into the soft mud around each plant.

For best results take lilies up and replant them every other year. Discard the old woody portion of the rootstock and replant the active "lead." Set rootstocks of tropical kinds just below the surface of the soil and the hardy water lilies about 1 inch deep.

Water lilies need full sun almost all day long.

Water poppy — *(Hydrocleys nymphoides)*. One of the best of the small aquatics is the water poppy. It looks like a miniature water lily, with yellow, poppy-like flowers coming in profusion all summer long. For pools too shallow for water lilies, water poppies are an excellent alternative, thriving in water 3 inches to a foot deep. A water poppy grows much like a strawberry plant, with runners thrown out from the base, on which form short petioles, leaves and flowers. Water poppies are easily increased by runners. Plant in a box or pool bottom. As previously noted, water poppies can also be used at the shallow edge of a pool.

Other landscaping ideas

Bamboo Background: Bamboo is a staple in pool landscaping. Not only is bamboo mirrored in a garden pool one of the most cooling sights imaginable, it adds an often desirable vertical dimension to a garden setting. Bamboo grows quickly and likes the moist soil of the pool area. It combines handsomely with elephant ears, and flowering ginger.

Bamboo will be an even more enjoyable plant if kept under control and this is best accomplished *before* planting. Tubs, pots, boxes, or raised beds will contain rampant growth, or use an 18-inch deep barrier of sheet metal, pressed asbestos or poured concrete bulkhead.

Among the many types of bamboo, several do especially well in the West and are well-suited to the pool garden.

Golden bamboo — *(Phyllostachys aurea)*. Grows as high as 30 feet, but usually much less. Stem diameter is 2 inches. Good screen for sun control, privacy. Does well in tubs.

Yellow groove bamboo—*(Phyllostachys aureosulcata)*. Very hardy runner. Hardy to —20°, a good one to try in cold areas. Grows to 30 feet with a diameter of 1½ inches.

Metake, arrow bamboo — *(Pseudosasa japonica)*. Grows to 18 feet; ¾ inch diameter. Stem sheaths never fall and plant sheds little.

Low bamboo — *(Sasa humilis)*. Ground cover that gets about 3 feet tall. Graceful arching stems. Rampant runner. Good in borders.

Dwarf bamboo — *(Sasa pygmaea)*. Good ground cover in fairly moist areas. Aggressive spreader. Grows 1 foot tall. If carefully contained, makes nice touches near pool.

Dwarfed pine dominates otherwise sparse planting around this tiny recreation of a high alpine pool.

C. Jacques Hahn design

Fitness of bamboo as a poolside plant is beautifully demonstrated in this garden, where tall and dwarf bamboo are flanked by podocarpus, juniper, and thuja.

These bamboos clump, rather than spread.

Fernleaf hedge bamboo — *(Bambusa multiplex* 'Fernleaf'). Narrow, closely spaced leaves, 10 to 20 per twig. Loses ferny quality in rich soil. Reaches 10 to 20 foot heights. Diameter, ½ inch.

Golden Goddess—*(Bambusa multiplex* 'Golden Goddess'). Similar to above but larger leaves and 8 to 10 foot height. Easy to control. Widely available. Hardy to 15°.

Alpine Pool Plants: There are endless alpine pool variations, here are some plant ideas to help create the alpine look:

Such dwarf false-cypress as *Chamaecyparis pisifera* 'Pygmaea' and *C. obtusa* 'Nana'; a good dwarf juniper like *Juniperus communis* 'Compressa'; such spruces as *Picea abies* 'Procumbens', *P. a.* 'Nidiformis', and *P. glauca* 'Conica'; arborvitae like *Thuja occidentalis* 'Globosa' (Tom Thumb arborvitae) and *T. orientalis* 'Nana'; the pines, Japanese black pine *(Pinus thunbergii)* and Mugho pine *(P. mugo mughus)*, which can be kept small.

Good ground covering shrubs are the heathers, kinnikinnick, salal, Point Reyes ceanothus *(C. gloriosus)*, lingonberry *(Vaccinium vitis-idaea)*, and longleaf mahonia *(M. nervosa)*.

These are fine for a spot of color: dwarf varieties of dianthus, rosy pink monkeyflower *(Mimulus lewisii)*, rockcress (Arabis), and draba.

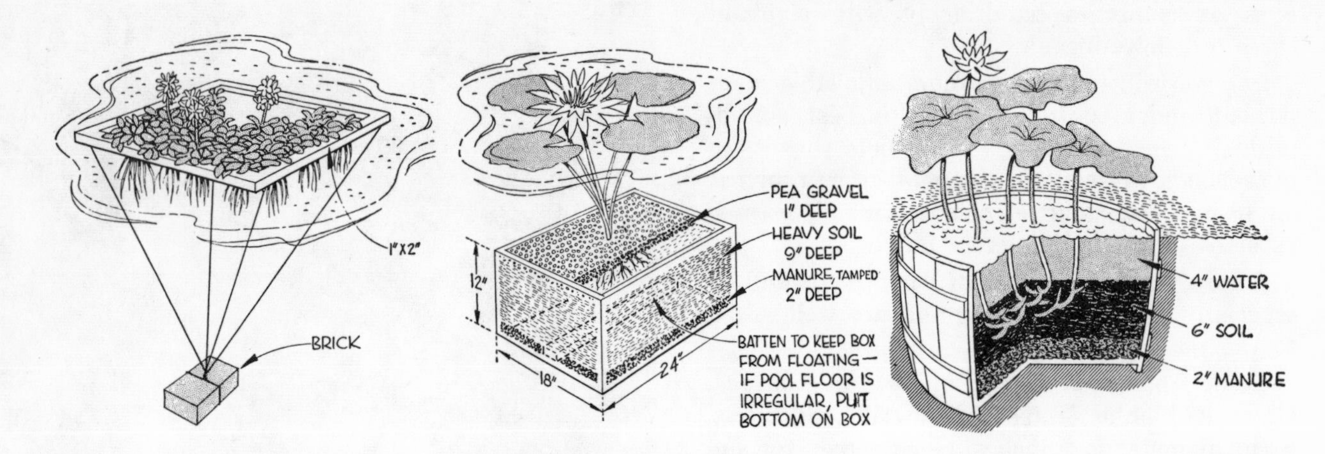

Continual drifting in wind causes water hyacinth to rot. Make a simple wood frame, moor by wires to brick.

Nail it together in a few minutes, using 1 by 12-inch pine. Mulch top with pea gravel if pool has big goldfish.

Sacred lotus becomes border plant in tub or half barrel either sunk in ground or placed above the ground.

Planting boxes: Use pine, *not redwood.* Redwood turns the water black and may kill both plants and fish. Use 1 by 12-inch stock; make boxes a foot deep and at least a foot square. Put 1 lily in each. Boxes 4 or 5 feet square will hold 2 or 3 lilies in each.

If the pool bottom is rounded, boxes should have a wooden floor. If bottom is flat, nail a 1 by 2-inch batten across the bottom, set the box on the floor of the pool and fill with planting mix.

For a planting mix use rich, heavy soil. Adobe is good. It can be enriched in either of two ways: (1) mix about ½ pound of commercial fertilizer into each wheelbarrow load of soil; or, (2) use manure (this is better).

Don't mix manure with the soil. It will decompose, bubble and foul the water. Instead, put 2 inches of manure in the bottom of the box, tamp it down firmly, then put 10 inches of soil on top. For a top dressing use coarse pea gravel. (Water lilies do not thrive in sand.)

Hyacinth frame: Make a small form of 1 by 2's, moor it to the bottom of the pool with wire and a brick, and put the clump of plants inside.

Lotus in half-barrel: Use a circular tub at least two feet in diameter in the ground or above ground. Fill within six inches of the top with manure and soil as prescribed for lilies. Plant lotus rootstocks horizontally in 1 to 2-inch deep trench. Leave growing tips showing. Keep tub filled to the top with water, but drain frequently until coloration from manure disappears and plants are established.

Photographer's credits

Ben Allen: page 24 (top), 44. Paul Aller: pages 65, 66. William Aplin: pages 15, 27, 28 (bottom), 29 (top l.), 35 (low l.), 75, 79. Aplin-Dudley Studios: pages 43 (top r.), 74, 78 (center, r.). Morley Baer: pages 9 (top l.), 15 (low l.), 25 (r.), 26 (l.), 33 (bottom), 39, 53 (l.). Baldinger Photo: page 30 (low r.). Mimi Bell: page 53 (top r.). Ernest Braun: pages 7 (r), 13 (low l., r.), 15 (low r.), 21 (low l., r.), 25 (low l.), 31 (bottom), 37, 38, 47 (l.), 52 (r.), 59 (r.), 71. Clyde Childress: pages 18, 20, 24 (bottom), 59 (l.), 70 (l.). Glenn Christiansen: page 54. Robert Cox: page 16. Virginia Davidson: page 17. Richard Dawson: pages 5 (r.), 21 (top l.), 34. Dearborn-Massar: page 70 (r.). Max Eckert: page 4. Richard Fish: pages 32 (top r., bottom), 48. Frank Gaynor: pages 28 (top), 35 (top l.). Sherry Gellner: page 55. Jeannette Grossman: page 46 (low l., low r.). Art Hupy: pages 25 (top l.), 43 (low r.), 50, 51, 68 (top). Tats Ishimoto: pages 40, 41. Eric Johnson: page 8 (l.). Don Knight: page 77 (l.). George Knight: page 30 (l.). Elsa Knoll: pages 7 (l.), 47 (low r.). Samson B. Knoll: pages 8 (cen. r.), 45. Roy Krell: page 12. Markow Photography: page 42 (l.). Jack McDowell: page 55 (bottom). Ken Molino: page 35 (r.). Joe Munroe: page 32 (top l.). Theodore Osmundson: pages 22, 23 (top), 29 (bottom). Rondal Partridge: pages 3, 46 (top). Tom Riley: pages 5 (l.), 14 (low l.), 23 (bottom), 29 (top r.), 52 (l.). John Robinson: pages 8 (top r.), 30 (top r.), 31 (top r.), 76 (r.), 77 (center, r.), 78 (r.). Julius Shulman: page 31 (top l.). William Steward: page 36. Darrow Watt: pages 6, 8 (low r.), 9 (top r.), 10, 19, 47 (top r.), 49, 67. R. Wenkam: pages 42 (r.), 68 (bottom). Alex Williams: page 43 (l.). Al Zelver: page 9 (low r.).